Paperbacks
in
Education

Paperbacks
in
Education

edited by Vivienne Anderson

Teachers College Press
Teachers College
Columbia University

Copyright © 1966 by Teachers College, Columbia University
Library of Congress Catalog Card Number: 66–19219
Manufactured in the United States of America
Cover design by Veit-Martin Associates
Second printing, 1966

Preface

WALTER CREWSON
*Associate Commissioner of Education,
New York State Education Department
and Chairman, Publications
Committee, Paperback Conference*

This conference, "The Role of Paperback Books in Education," held at Teachers College, Columbia University, from October 7–9, 1965, was an organized effort to recognize the importance of providing broad avenues for accommodating the flow of the accumulated and expanding knowledge and wisdom of mankind to oncoming generations.

The paperback book serves a unique purpose in this vital cause. It is inexpensive, thus available in quantity to many students and teachers who are not favorably enough situated to secure such materials in more permanent form. Its inexpensiveness opens the door to a massive broadening of available offerings for the enrichment of curriculum and for serving the individual needs of students having an infinite range of capacities and interests.

Let us hope that such conferences will be widely held, that the entire education profession may be alerted to the infinite variety of excellent teaching tools made possible by the paperback book.

And let us express appreciation at this time to the Committee of Forty—leading educators and publishing officials—who worked in dedicated fashion to plan this international conference.

The Committee of Forty

PROJECT COORDINATOR

DR. VIVIENNE ANDERSON, New York State Education Department and Teachers College

EXECUTIVE COMMITTEE

Co-chairmen

DR. NORTON BEACH
Professor of Education, Teachers College

WILLIAM D. BOUTWELL
Editorial Vice President, Scholastic Magazines and Book Services

DR. ROBERT SHAFER
Associate Professor of English, Teachers College

Other Members

DR. HENRY M. BRICKELL
Educational Testing Service, Princeton
Assistant Superintendent, Manhasset

MRS. CHARLOTTE BROOKS
Supervising Director, Department of English, Washington Public Schools

ALEXANDER BUTMAN
Director, Education Department Bantam Books, Inc.

DR. WALTER CREWSON
Associate Commissioner, New York State Education Department

NORMAN ELMES
Educational Director, Dell Publishing Company, Inc.

FRANK G. JENNINGS
Education Consultant, New World Foundation

PYKE JOHNSON, JR.
Editor-in-Chief, Anchor Books

HAROLD H. LASKEY
Paperback Exhibits Director
The Combined Book Exhibit, Inc.

ROBERT LOCKE
Vice-President, College Division McGraw-Hill Book Company

DR. JOSEPH O. LORETAN
Deputy Superintendent
New York City Public Schools

MRS. JOHN MALLORY
President, New York State Congress of Parents and Teachers

SISTER M. SYLVIA, S.S.J.
Victory Academy, Lackawanna N. Y.

JOHN WARE
Educational Director, Pocket Books, Inc.

PLANNING COMMITTEES

Program

DR. JOSEPH O. LORETAN
Chairman

DR. LLOYD ASHBY
Superintendent of Schools
Ridgewood, New Jersey

DR. NORTON BEACH

WILLIAM D. BOUTWELL

DR. HENRY M. BRICKELL

ALEXANDER BUTMAN

DR. MORRIS GALL
Norwalk Public Schools
Connecticut

JOHN KOONTZ
Assistant Superintendent, Public Schools, District of Columbia

ABRAHAM LASS
Principal, Abraham Lincoln High School, Brooklyn, New York

vii

FRANK McLAUGHLIN
Monmouth Regional High School
New Shrewsbury, New Jersey
SISTER MARY NORA, S.S.N.D.
Associate Secretary, Elementary
School Department, The National
Catholic Educational Association
DAVID SOHN
Darien Public Schools
Connecticut
DR. M. JERRY WEISS
Jersey City State College
MISS ELINOR YUNGMEYER,
Libraries, Oak Park Elementary
Schools, Illinois
DAVID ZAMCHICK
Great Neck Public Schools

Publicity
FRANK G. JENNINGS
Co-chairman
HAROLD H. LASKEY
Co-chairman
ROBERT LOCKE
DR. SIDNEY FORMAN
Professor of Education and Li-
brarian, Teachers College
Columbia University

Publication
DR. WALTER CREWSON
Chairman
DR. MAX BOGART
Assistant Director, Division of
Curriculum and Instruction, New
Jersey State Department of Edu-
cation
S. ALAN COHEN
Director of Reading, Mobilization
for Youth, New York City

DR. SIDNEY DORROS
Director, Publications Division
National Education Association
LOUIS A. FANGET
Chief, Publications Division
United States Information Agency
DR. JAMES HALL
Superintendent of Schools
Port Washington, New York
DR. ARNO JEWETT
Chief, English and Foreign Lan-
guage Section, U. S. Office of
Education
PYKE JOHNSON, JR.
HAROLD M. LONG
Glens Falls High School
Glens Falls, New York
DR. ROBERT SHAFER

Exhibitions and Utilization
MRS. CHARLOTTE BROOKS
Chairman
MRS. MARY CHILDS
The Children's Book Council, Inc.
NORMAN ELMES
DR. RAY TRAUTMAN
Professor, School of Library
Service, Columbia University
JOHN WARE

Hospitality
MRS. JOHN MALLORY
Co-chairman
SISTER M. SYLVIA, S.S.J.
Co-chairman
AUSTIN FOX
Nichols School, Buffalo, New
York
DR. DEBORAH WOLFE
Professor of Education, Queens
College

Messages from the Cosponsoring Publishing Groups

DAN LACY
Managing Director,
American Book Publishers Council

The American Book Publishers Council is pleased to have been asked to cosponsor the conference, "The Role of Paperback Books in Education," at Teachers College, Columbia University. This international conference—the first of its kind —brought together publishers and educators who are concerned with the wider and wiser use of books to enrich and strengthen the instructional program and, therefore, help to broaden the educational experience of students of all ages.

The "paperback revolution," as it has been called, has made available to students and general readers a body of book information which previously had been difficult to procure. It has also challenged the talents of publishers in their work as editors, designers and distributors and has stimulated all educators to develop new ways of using a wider range of books and of leading students to more independent and individualized study. And now we are witnessing the use of paperback children's books for readers in the elementary grades.

This wider use of books has brought changes in techniques of book selection and purchase, circulation, use and sale of books. Discussion here of many of these changes reflects a growing awareness among publishers of the needs of educators and among educators of the workings of the publishing industry. The use of books in all areas of the curriculum and in special programs—such as those to reach slower readers, the culturally disadvantaged, and accelerated students—is expanding rapidly. With increased federal, state, and local aid to schools and libraries, more and more students will grow to be better readers and, ultimately, better citizens.

The Council congratulates you on your attention to all these important concerns and trusts that the channels of communication opened and widened at this conference will continue to be useful and effective.

AUSTIN J. McCAFFREY
Executive Director,
American Textbook Publishers Institute

The use of paperbacks as instructional tools is so new that we are just beginning to understand the paperback's relationship to the textbook. We have only begun to explore the fruitful ways in which paperbacks can enrich and broaden the school curriculum. This first international paperback conference, which the American Textbook Publishers Institute was happy to cosponsor, is a public recognition on the part of both educators and publishers that the paperback is an important teaching and learning tool, and that it has a significant contribution to make to American education.

We have been describing the advent of paperbacks in the classroom as a "paperback revolution." Perhaps we would be more accurate in describing it as a revolution in education, since it is the increasing number of new concepts in methodology and learning patterns that has created a role for the paperback in our schools. It is a truism that each cultural period develops the materials best suited to its particular needs, and in so doing creates the mechanisms of dynamic change that finally alter the established cultural patterns themselves. The development of the paperback, along with other printed materials and new technological devices for the classroom, illustrates an increasing awareness of the expanding needs and changing nature of our society.

Our progress, prosperity, and security depend, in large part, upon the quality and amount of effort we devote to raising the cultural and skill standards of our educable citizens. Education must cope simultaneously with the explosive demands of a rapidly increasing population, new curricular needs in terms of a highly sophisticated technology and the proliferation of new knowledges at an unbelievable rate. In order to do this, educators must explore new avenues of approach to old and familiar problems. They must re-examine the learning process, adapt new methodologies, and investigate new systems of learning and the multi-use of all kinds of instructional materials.

In this respect, this first international paperback conference is of great importance, since it has brought educators and publishers together to explore a promising new development in the range of instructional materials.

What Next?

VIVIENNE ANDERSON

*Chief, Bureau of Continuing Education Curriculum Development,
New York State Education Department and
Coordinator, Paperback Conference,
Teachers College, Columbia University*

The above question was asked by many eager and hopeful conference participants. Teachers College had organized and conducted a three-day international conference; teams of educators (500 of them) from over thirty states, the District of Columbia, more than twenty of our largest cities, and Canada had met with representatives of approximately 120 publishing companies to scrutinize the unique contribution of paperback books in the schools of today and their potential role in the educational program of the future.

The conference was cosponsored by Teachers College, Columbia University, the American Book Publishers Council, and the American Textbook Publishers Institute, under a grant from the New World Foundation. For the first time, a major international forum was provided for leaders from education and the publishing world to examine candidly and realistically the development of paperback books as a medium for enriching the school program.

This report—a paperback book, of course—presents the major conference addresses; a synthesis of fifty-two discussion sessions relating to paperbacks in all major phases of the curriculum, as well as administrative and selection policies; case studies illustrating the effective use of paperbacks; a background article; and a selected bibliography of writings on paperback books. No separate section is included on research since two of the three major research studies to this date—those conducted in New York City and the state of New Jersey—are described in this book by Dr. Joseph Loretan and Dr. Max

Bogart. The third study of national repute—the Texas study— examined the relative durability of the hardcover and the paperback textbook and reported the greater durability of the hardcover book.

But, What Next?

Let us get back to the original question and examine what has happened since the conference took place. Teachers College has taken the following steps to insure some degree of continuity for the widescale exploration of paperbacks initiated at the conference. A continuing program will be charted by Professor Sidney Forman, Teachers College Librarian. The initial stages of this program will focus on the following activities:

1. The formation of a Teachers College committee, involving personnel from the Department of Curriculum and Teaching and the Institute of Educational Technology, to formulate general policy for the paperback program and to channel information about the project to classes.
2. The creation of a paperback display and information center in the Teachers College Library, providing published information on paperbacks: their history, production, distribution and use in the curriculum.

Future problems which may be examined at Teachers College include techniques of budgeting for paperbacks in schools, methods of distribution, and the role of libraries in the paperback field.

Books for Mass Culture

Looking beyond the College itself for a moment, paperback books are already becoming effective instruments in broadening a national cultural appetite. The small, easy-to-carry, easy-to-read, softcover book has gained a universal popularity that removes the "egghead" stigma from the printed volume. Over thirty-five thousand titles are now available with four thousand of these suitable for school use and fifty new ones, appropriate for education, being released every month.

Teachers and administrators should remember that federal funds can be used profitably for the significant enrichment of school and classroom libraries through the purchase of a wide variety of paperbacks as well as hardcover books. Title II of the Elementary and Secondary Education Act of 1965, in particular, provides specifically for the purchase of printed materials which can be used by schools to build increased literacy and readership along with better standards of taste and appreciation. Title I of the same Act provides the opportunity to acquire books and other published materials for the culturally deprived as well as to employ professional librarians, library aids and reading specialists to insure the proper and effective use of these printed materials with these students.

These federal funds can also be used to great advantage for the purchase of paperbacks and other printed materials designed for the professional growth of the teaching and administrative staff—a pressing need which alert teachers and administrators are anxiously seeking to satisfy because of the overwhelming demands of new content and pioneering techniques in education.

A Breakthrough

The noticeable arrival of the paperback book on the education scene is particularly timely. It comes during a period when a long tradition of unbending rigidity in the education structure is being challenged. The traditional grouping of thirty pupils per teacher is beginning to give way to larger and smaller groups —even independent individual study and research. Curriculum content is reaching toward younger students: College subjects are being taught in advanced placement courses in high school; large segments of high school content are shifting to the junior high; junior high content is moving into the elementary grades. This "downward movement" creates an urgent demand for greater specialization of knowledge on the part of the teacher, with a resulting merging of teacher talents through team arrangements, and increased flexibility in scheduling because of new variations in class size, structure, and purpose.

These emerging patterns inevitably require a wider, richer assortment of books and materials to enhance both the student's program and the informational and professional background of the teacher and the administrator. In mass education, as in the population in general, individual differences demand printed materials which provide variety in content, length, complexity, and readability.

What next? Let us hope that through the continued program at Teachers College and through the acts of many interested educators and laymen, the relatively low-cost paperback book will be used to create new patterns of searching and learning for pupils and teachers, and will improve the readership, scholarship and tastes of students in school and laymen in the community.

Contents

PANEL DISCUSSIONS

GROUP DISCUSSIONS

CASE STUDIES

THE FUTURE

SELECTED BIBLIOGRAPHY

MAJOR ADDRESSES

Reading and Thinking

HAROLD TAYLOR
Educator and Lecturer

I should apologize at the outset for the fact that I thought my invitation was to speak on hardcover publications, and I therefore prepared a fifty-minute statement on rare books and first editions, arguing that fly-by-night paperback publishers are intruding on our traditional literary values. However, since no person who presents himself to an audience should come without at least three speeches, I happen to have a contrary statement which begins by saying that the mass introduction of low-cost books to the public has had the same effect on the world of culture that the atomic bomb has had on the conduct of military strategy, although the news has not reached educators as yet. There will be a series of dull thuds as the fallout hits education during the next five years.

I speak, therefore, in favor of mass culture, on the simple ground that, when there is more of it to go around, the percentage is raised of those who are able to understand values, ideas, and aesthetic objects. I would like to deal with the mass distribution of low-cost books as one aspect of the spread of mass culture, and to express great joy that so many books are getting around, and presumably being read. I would like to consider the phenomena of mass culture as one aspect of the liberation of the individual. This is an unpopular view. I see mass culture not as a curse on the society, as a decline of art, or as evidence of the tyranny of the American middle class. I will confess at the outset to a weariness of hearing, from critics of the culture, that too many people are getting into it, just as I tend to weary very quickly when I hear people talk about there being too many students in the colleges and universities and about mass education only diluting the quality of education itself. When the colleges fail, it is more often because those who work

3

in the field of education have not been attending to their true task—the education of students. The general thesis among those who reject the culture of the masses is that whatever was once a private matter for an élite and which, later on, becomes a private matter for millions, is somehow debased in the process.

Among those who have detected a general decline in the culture in recent years are those who, like Jacques Barzun, deplore the thickening up of a bureaucratic society whose universities have become bureaucractic corporations, thus guaranteeing the decline of the liberal arts and the destruction of sensibility. Mr. Barzun, in an address two years ago at a nearby institution, noted that so many students are now married, employed, going to or returning from conferences, "apprehensive about examinations, ruled by the clock like the most harried executives," that they are not cloistered within the walls of the academies but are out in the midst of society which is why, said Mr. Barzun, so many of them are in the midst of psychiatric treatment. From a different perspective one might take an opposite view and say that the educators who lay the traps for students by constantly testing them, running them from class to class at the ringing of bells, organizing the daylights out of the entire curriculum, sitting on the students' heads, and not letting them up, are in fact killing the spirit and the enjoyment of the liberal arts at the very time the educators deplore the loss of their vitality. Where does the vitality of the liberal arts come from, if not from the minds and hearts of the students?

The problem of a mass culture, as far as the arts and sciences are concerned, is simple: it is to make it possible for each person in the culture to become directly involved in the arts and sciences, at whatever level a beginning may be made. The colleges and universities have no special prerogatives here, although they incline to act as if they had, to keep the true cultural values within their walls, dispensing these values a little bit at a time in three lectures a week on payment of the proper tuition. The mass availability of books now makes obsolete most of the ideas and practices of the schools and universities, including the concept which Jules Feiffer refers to as the concept of the concentrated cultural zoo.

"While the rest of our landscape uglies up," says Mr. Feiffer, "we are anxious to build a place (*some* place) that is pretty, an *official* pretty, a pretty we can go to, pay a dollar to, come home from, and say, 'Yes, I have seen pretty. It is there.' The more ugly life gets outside our windows, the more anxious we are to contain beauty elsewhere; a tree inside a fence, a bird inside a sanctuary, an artist inside a zoo. Aware of our impulse mainly to destroy, we cage those things we think it desirable to save. What we leave on the outside is show business, portraits of lonely artists discussing their alienation in full-color picture-books or with David Susskind on television."

What we also leave on the outside is a popular culture, rooted in the lusty, the noisy, the boisterous, and the vulgar. I would like to draw your attention to the fact that the term vulgar has to do with the size of the crowd of persons who are behaving rather than the actual things they are doing. What is needed in our cultural institutions is the vitality of the vulgar with the quality of the sensitive. It is not impossible to combine these two. What was called vulgar in the middle of the nineteenth century by certain astute members of the élite suddenly became the art of the late nineteenth century in the hands of the middle class. Progress in society is made by those who do not have the good taste not to say what they think and who do such out-rageous things as overthrowing their governments, shooting up their generals, and in general asserting freedoms which are not freely given to them. These are vulgar acts by rude people. On the other hand, they do get done some things which sadly need doing.

I did not come before you to plead with you on behalf of the vulgar, but I think we might redefine the term so that those in the community who have vulgar tendencies may feel free to express themselves. I draw attention to the fact that those who are called cultural deviants and delinquents in our society comprise within their ranks some of the most difficult and interesting people we have in America. We are discovering a number of things about them as we turn our attention to the problems of poverty and to other problems stirred up by Mr. Johnson in his effort to achieve a consensus within all of America. As we look at the cultures which have been hidden beneath the assumption that middle-class, white values are the supreme ideal for America, we are finding that in every segment of the newly discovered society there are persons whose ideas and possibilities so outrun anything we already possess in the established culture as to be astonishing.

In some ways we have already managed to achieve a degree of integration of the vulgar and the sensitive in the modified vulgarity of pop art, and in the transformation of reality in the art of the happening. Here both art and reality are redefined so that art can use all reality and all reality is capable of becoming art. This, it seems to me, is a genuinely new factor in contemporary culture, related to massive changes in technology and changes in mass attitudes towards what the arts can be. The fact is that the popular culture *has* started movements toward an interest in the arts, and that the ultimate vulgarity of commercial entertainment on television will find itself modified by such influences as the effect of new reading habits and a wider reading public, created by the spread of low-cost books.

You are familiar, I am sure, with the arithmetic of the situation. There were 35,500 paperback titles in 1965, as against a mere 5,500 in 1960. One third of the entire market in paperbacks is in the educational field. The impact on the publications industry and on those elements which can be designated as aspects of mass culture has been extraordinary. The astonishing fact is that the paperback achieves a life of its own, regardless of what the hardcover books do. I will leave to others the tracing out of the economic intricacies of this new reform within the culture. It does mean, however, that there are economic forces at least consciously working on behalf of mass culture, and I think it is to the credit of the education industry that it should now have combined forces with the economic industries of a more conventional kind. The shift is away from the conception of the book as an object only to be treasured by those who have custody of them intellectually or personally into the idea of the book as a usable instrument for the extension of one's experience into new modes. One sees fifteen- and sixteen-year-old boys in the subway reading books unashamedly, books they would not have been reading ten or fifteen years ago, simply because the conception of having a book of one's own has shifted. It has shifted away from the notion that a book is something which certain classes of people have in their libraries at home whereas the rest of the world does not buy them, does not read them.

A new generation has grown up in the period of mass communication, and the effects upon the mass sensibility have as yet been little observed. Already I have seen a change in the attitude of college students and high school students toward their curriculum, a change which I believe can be traced directly to the impact of the paperback movement on young readers. Books which in former years were hidden away in public libraries or embalmed in college curricula are now out in the open and are being read by high school students before they reach college. A new college student generation which has found its own identity through political, social, and intellectual action has found it in part by the reading it has done in a wide new field, from contemporary novels and the manuals on sex, which in some cases cannot be distinguished, to the classics of literary history which mingle with everything else on the drugstore racks and in the supermarkets. Although the makers of freshman curricula have not noticed this fact, the students have simply gone past the customary texts and have started on their own. They have drawn together a body of knowledge which comprises the culture of the enlightened young.

This has induced new attitudes which appear in those clusters of new values which go together to produce the Berkeley revolt, which go together to produce on nearly every campus in the country a new and more mature attitude toward education. On the basis of new reading, in previous years unavailable, on the basis of new effects from the public affairs programs of television, from the new effects of mass distribution of short stories and articles in the picture magazines, there has developed a sophistication on the part of the younger generation which is reflected in the attitude they take to the education they get.

At a college which tries to be sensible about its curriculum (and I mention one at random—Sarah Lawrence) the observation of what the students are capable of reading and what they have already read is a determining factor in what is put into the curriculum. This seems to be a basic, simple fact of educational policy which should be shared by all those who plan the education of the young. In fact, this is still a radical idea in curriculum making, and the fact that Sarah Lawrence College refuses to administer grades or to have examinations or to have a set of required courses for all is still a radical approach to the whole field of education.

The high visibility now being given to the protest movement among the young for civil rights for the Negro has obscured the fact that the protest is also being made against the idea of the cultural authority of the university which, in the students' view, has no right to impose banalities and aesthetic tedium on the student body. We need to pay serious attention to the fact that many of the available ideas which come to the latter years of the high school student and to the new generation of college students, come because of the emancipation from curricula which now become available to him through the massive spread of low-cost books.

Those critics of the mass culture, who use such terms as midcult and low-cult and all the other cults except the one that the person is writing in, hold the notion that as we spread culture through the masses it becomes thinner. There is a curious metaphor there, as if culture were a substance of which there is only a certain amount and, since there is only a certain amount the right people have it and, if you are lucky they will spread a little of it around to the masses. There is a basic flaw in the metaphor. What is happening is that as the popular culture affects the young, the middle aged, and the others through the atrocities of television, through the spread of the mass magazines and the mass media, of which the paperback book is one component, it is as if a whole new series of persons who never before had their own place in the culture have now been introduced one at a time to books, to imagery, to world affairs, to a new reality.

There are a number of unobserved facts which may account in the future for what we can hope will be a maturing of the popular culture in America. It is no accident that across the country we have an extraordinary degree of interest in the performing arts, in the visual arts, and in a whole new area of cultural values. It is not without significance that we have now had, for the first time in American history, a bill passed by Congress on behalf of the arts and the humanities. I should think that this, interpreted in a certain way, is not only an expression of Mr. Johnson's wish to cover all electoral fronts (if there are any voters among the poets, he wants them too), but also represents a surge of interest from beneath. In one sense it is the popular culture asserting itself and saying to its government, "It is time that we all had a chance at the arts."

I would not like to push this thesis too far, since the process by which that bill was introduced and passed is very complicated. Let me put it this way. As the philosophers are fond of saying, what we have here is a necessary but not adequate condition for the development of an enormous expansion of American culture. The signing of the bill, in other words, is symbolic of the recognition of the needs of the society for a cultural future.

All the things which can be lumped together under the term *mass media* and the mass cultural apparatus have combined to produce a new attitude toward culture. But something else has happened. It is the effect of the speed of publication of the facts about the society, the presentation in visual and written form of events so soon after they occur, upon a public understanding of the events themselves. Perhaps the most dramatic personal experience this country has undergone since Mr. Roosevelt's announcement of the declaration of war was the assassination of Mr. Kennedy. In no previous era in American history was it possible so to arrange the publication and the extension of a public event so directly into the lives of the American people immediately and simultaneously, through television, radio and press, and immediately to sum up the tragedy, to put it in context, to examine what it was by having available to a wide segment of the American people paperback books containing documents, written accounts by personal friends, and any amount of other material.

A change in the quality of the American political process is also being achieved by the technology of book publication. The speed of publication of the materials related to the Berkeley student revolt of last year will have an important impact on cultural and educational changes on the campuses across the country during this present year. Formerly we would have had to wait so long for the documents and analyses that the issues themselves would have been forgotten and the interest in them diminished.

The mass production of the automobile revolutionized American culture and American society and developed new attitudes to nearly every aspect of American life by opening up the country to itself. The mobility of the population assured a reaching out and a coming back of all elements in the society. Similarly, the availability of these instruments of communication to a wide sector of the American people will have effects which, at present, are unpredictable but which will certainly change the society.

Those of you who are teachers here and those of you who are working directly with schools are aware of the valuable developments in the paperback libraries and of the ways in which enlightened people can expand their own work in the curriculum itself. I don't think in my whole life I have ever had the courage to spend one hundred dollars on books all at once in one bookstore. In my family we grew up in a sterile culture and a book was something that was kept in a library by formidable custodians, and there were certain rules and regulations made which always made it impossible for you to read the book you wanted. The attitude to books themselves was not one which would encourage you to put them high on your shopping list. Food was the major problem in the family budget, since my father showed his lack of enterprise by being unemployed during the depression. The family tended not to pay attention to the higher values, as they are called, and I grew up having to finish everything on my plate and not buy books.

This past year I was about to lecture on philosophical and educational questions in Turkey, Greece, and Iran at the universities, and it was suggested by the State Department that I take with me some paperback books which I could distribute to anyone who might be interested. I went to a paperback bookstore and, for the first time in my life, I had the extraordinary joy which only comes from being able to get the things you have always wanted. For one hundred dollars I found that I had many, many of the things which I had half read in the past and others that I had always wanted to read. My problem then became not only that of getting the books to Greece, Turkey, and Iran but, once taking them there, of not refusing to give them up.

I find more and more people in this country who share my kind of attitude toward books. They want to own them so that they can read them on their own time, when they feel like it. One of the major problems in America is with the educators who, as I have suggested at the beginning of my talk, possess ideas which are in large part obsolete. The temptation of the educator is not to leave the books alone, not to let the writer of the book speak to the student himself, but always to intervene, to describe, to explain, to organize a body of knowledge for the student, leaving the student with very little to do. I have never been able to understand why educators do this, especially when books and art objects are concerned. Much of the time they force their students to read the wrong books, at the wrong time, in the wrong way. That is, they choose a list of books by academic experts who have divided knowledge into departments the better to manage it, and they lecture to the students about what is in the books, they reduce the content of books to a series of points which can be numbered, and are numbered, and if there are discussions, the discussions are always to deal with the points that are numbered. Those of you who are teachers, who have looked into the notebooks of your students, will find there a kind of mathematical approach to whatever you have said.

I know that in some of my most brilliant lectures in philosophy at the University of Wisconsin I found various series of numbers with statements which I swear I never made and some of the most beautiful drawings of Plato and Aristotle in full color which you would ever come across. The schools and the colleges deliberately empty the books of their content, they empty the art objects of their true meaning, and they addict their students to habits of thought that often last for the rest of their lives. Everything must be placed in a summary. Ideas are topic sentences. To read is not really to read, it is to prepare for a distant test. This is why so many people simply don't know how to read. They have been taught to turn books into digests of information. When they were students they learned to get rid of their books as soon as the semester was over; you've seen them doing it. They run straight to the bookstore to sell, not to buy, books. It is perfectly natural. Having been used, the books, like paper cups, are no longer useful.

The heart of education where books are concerned is to get the student alone with a book in a right state of mind, that is to say receptive, interested, curious, involved, or, if possible, possessed, by the book. I have never been able to understand why educators do not seize on this simple fact and make it the center of their educational planning. Why do they not make one life of the double life students lead, rather than forcing them to find their intellectual and personal interests outside the organized curriculum? Indeed, the students are too often made to read more than they can ever enjoy, and yet too little of too many things, in a way calculated to destroy direct involvement with the writer.

In the case of textbooks, it is impossible to find the writer. I would be prepared to say that there is no good textbook, but I would not like to urge it on this audience. The textbook has its use in holding the system of education together. Without the textbook the teachers would fall apart, it is said, and nothing would happen. A textbook is a way of making knowledge safe from the teacher.

Under the present system, the brighter the students the more they are asked to read. As the incoming students at Harvard University have become brighter because of reading illegally in high school, they have outrun the capacities of the faculty in many respects, and the response of the faculty has been to make longer assignments to keep the students so busy that they will not be able to think about what they have read. Some students, not necessarily in the Ivy League but right across the country, have developed prodigious skills in reading fast and cleverly and sprinkling their papers with quotations which advertise their wealth of coverage. The duller the students, the shorter the assignment. Half-chapters or a certain number of pages at a time. The more the textbooks provided for the dull ones, the more the anthologies, the more the course outlines, the more the objective examinations, the more chance there is that, if you are not dull and academic when you come in, the university will make you that way.

When I say dull, I do not mean that there is something wrong with students who are so classified, I mean that students have not been taught to read in depth or to be interested in reading as a form of enlightenment and enjoyment. Average students are exactly the ones who would profit most by learning to read for joy. That idea in education seems to have slipped away from the educators. Why not put into the hands of students those books which are nonacademic? Most of the books which students are asked to read in college are anti-intellectual in their effects. Students, bright or dull, are always reading to a deadline, to return books to the library, to prepare for tests, to pass the course, and there is never enough time to do more than to read the amount of the author the assignment allows.

I spent a week on an eastern campus some time ago, as a visiting educator, and had a chance to see at first hand the work of the administration, faculty, and students. I found the freshmen and sophomores completely encased in the heaviest set of course requirements I have come across in a long time. I was able to express this feeling of academic constriction publicly to the faculty and student body at several meetings, and I found one student who said that if you miss cleaning your teeth in the morning, you were through for the day since there was no chance in the schedule to add an extra five minutes.

I had the privilege of lunching on successive days with freshmen, sophomores, juniors, and seniors, and I found that the liveliest ones were in the freshman year and that those who had been on campus for three years seemed to be less interesting. One young man asked me at lunch (he was a certified sophomore) if I ever met, in my visits to colleges, any unofficial students, and I replied that I could not tell unofficial students from any other kind and that I met whoever was around. The young man said that he knew where there were some students who seldom came out into the open but who had some ideas I might not otherwise come across.

At around 1 A.M. the next morning, I found myself discussing literature and the fine arts with a group of five or six students who had very strong views about education, their own and that of others. "We used to be able to write easily in high school, but now we find it very hard; we have had all these English courses." They referred to the sense of being locked into the curriculum, always having to read from a sense of duty, and having to read so much, the length of the reading assignments having increased to match the level of their intellectual capability, that they had all their time occupied by assignments and literally had no time to think about what they were reading. One of the boys said, "What I need to do most, at this time in my life, is to read Paul Tillich. I read a little of him in last week's assignment, and he is saying something to me which no one has ever said before. But I can't read him unless I stay up all night, and then I won't be ready for my class tomorrow because I'll read Tillich."

I encouraged him to defy the system and read Tillich.

On the part of the educators, there has been a refusal to come to terms with the reality of the student's experience as a reader, a refusal to look at those unconscious processes which only take place when the objective phenomena of life are set aside for a while; in those moments in time when there is nothing at stake, when there is nothing scheduled, when one's mind and heart and body have a chance to walk along on their own and when the fortuitous and the accidental are freely accepted, when the idiosyncratic can arise in the place of the conventional. This is a crucially important point, particularly in relation to possibilities in educational planning.

Now that we have what amounts to the full panoply of literature before us, in every field of human knowledge, the entire apparatus of learning is open to us in fresh and fascinating ways. We can, for example, look at the means through which the sort of free and flexible assignments which are possible to teachers of literature can entrance the student by having him read things which get him excited about literature, without regard to whether or not this may at this moment in time be considered to be great literature. Greatness is not perceived by the young until they have first had the experience of a literary or intellectual kind which can make the student respond to the reading itself. To become lost in the reading, to disappear into the writer's mind, and to come out on the other side enriched by that passage—this is what we should be trying to accomplish for the student, not loading him up with more assignments. It is particularly reprehensible that this should be the familiar mode of curriculum planning at a time when we can now break loose from all the inhibitions.

Regarding those who are today to become engineers or doctors, or professionals of any kind, there is another kind of curriculum planning which I would like to draw to your attention—the pre-courses. You always take pre-engineering courses, pre-medical courses, pre-something or other, and there is no room left, not even for the sad little survey, for anything else but the requirements for the chosen profession. Jack Gelber, whom you will know as the author of *The Connection*, received a university education which had nothing at all to do with his intellectual development and less than nothing to do with his later career as a playwright. "I was a chemistry major, at first," he said, "thinking I'd be a chemist or a chemical engineer. Then I wound up studying journalism, which dealt mainly with how to get a job in radio and television. Which I didn't want. Within two weeks after graduation, I got a lift in a friend's car to San Francisco. I had one hundred dollars saved from working summers as a sheet metal worker and when that ran out I got a job as a ship fitter's helper. . . ."

Gelber's account of himself goes on to indicate that he met a number of interesting people in San Francisco, got involved with the whole movement in poetry and free-hand reading, and learning by thinking, outside the California universities, walking the streets of New York, and seeing a great many movies. Then he began writing his first play. After the success of the

play he was asked about his literary influences, and this is what
he replied: "I haven't read too much, but at the University of
Illinois I had a job in the library, where I came across a lot of
things that interested me. The Books of the Dead, Egyptian and
Tibetan, that give advice to people who die. Early Greek philosophy. I've been attracted to Turgenev, Gorki, Gogol. I
never really read Proust, but I read Rilke and the German ex-
pressionists of the twenties. *Alexanderplatz, Berlin,* and *The
Sleepwalkers* had a great effect on me. In the library, I first
got interested in Buddhism. I've always had a great interest in
religious states of being. That little baby in there knows everything right now that he's ever going to know, but some day it
will all be revealed to him. That's the way I was in the library.
I was in a conducive state. I wanted to know."

It is crucially important to note that this discursive reading,
which had nothing to do with Mr. Gelber's education, was the
most important thing that happened to him during the whole
of his stay at the University of Illinois. Although it is not necessary to argue that the University of Illinois should entirely have
revised its curricula in order to arrange that those who begin in
chemistry should be prepared as dramatists, it seems to me
that the least the university could have done was to get Mr.
Gelber into the library in a conducive state of mind without
actually paying him to go there as an assistant. It is entirely
probable that if Mr. Gelber had not had to work in the library,
and had not had the freedom of the stacks, he would never have
learned to read.

I should like to mention two practical items in the mass
availability of books. There is really no longer any need in the
high school, elementary school, or college curriculum for con-
stricted planning of the sort we now have, unless we are concerned to produce a faculty-proof curriculum which cannot be
damaged by the teacher. We need to reform the education of
teachers in such a way that the teachers would later refuse to
accept anyone else's curriculum and would be the first to search
through the entire available literature for new works, for new
materials, for new things which lie outside the products of the
textbook manufacturers, the film-strip makers, and those who

package knowledge for you without your needing to interfere with its process. We need to look at how one could, with the use of paperbacks, teach the conventional course in philosophy.

I can recall that, in teaching philosophy at the University of Wisconsin, I was restricted in the things which I could do with my students, not only by the intellectual and cultural deprivations they had suffered in high school but by the incapacity of students to be sufficiently interested in the books we were reading, to buy them for themselves, or even to go through the trouble of trying to get one of the six reserve copies in the library. We who are teachers have all had the experience of having to face honestly the fact that no assignment we could make could in good faith be carried out by the students to whom we were making the assignment, because it was physically impossible for them to carry out an assignment on a basis other than a quick run-through. Some of us anticipated the paperback movement by having everything around mimeographed, with or without copyright, and some of us were even reduced to writing things ourselves, in the absence of available books that spoke sense on the subject.

I discovered, in preparation for my talk this evening, a list of books which are provocative in their mere listing and which, had they been available at the time I was teaching philosophy, would not only have suggested to me things I had not thought of doing, but would have made available to my students such a wide variety of philosophical experience that many of them could have conducted research projects, written term papers, conducted discussions, and dealt with issues which would not be available under any system except one which allowed them to own their own books.

Consider, for example, the availability of Mercea Eliade's book, *The Myth of the Eternal Return,* which breaks new ground in the conception of philosophy itself. That book, costing eight or nine dollars and held by the librarian, would have been unavailable to me as a teacher. Or consider the availability of Freud's *On Creativity and the Unconscious*—papers on the psychology of art, literature, love, and religion; that is one book I wanted to use in my aesthetics course, but I could not assign it because there was only one copy in the University of Wisconsin library, and certainly the library could not switch its arrangements so that all the books bought on the budget over the next three years were going to be books in aesthetics for that particular philosophy course.

As one goes down similar lists of paperbacks, it is stimulating to the teacher to see what one could do in the construction of new courses, which one knows would be provocative for the students one is teaching. I suggest that this has the seed in it of a revolution in curriculum making, if those in the teachers' colleges can reshape the mode of teaching in order to train the student to become an independent scholar and an independent curriculum maker through new paperback possibilities. The textbooks are needed, in some cases, as reference books, but the original works are the only things which really matter, if we are concerned with creating a continuing interest in reading and thinking on the part of students after they leave college.

Such documents as the Moynihan report on the Negro family are now immediately available. Public documents which formerly were in the hands of government officials and released only after they were first published by the government, are now being arranged for joint publication and become accessible to the general public. The Moynihan report is a good example. Here was a document whose content had such direct relevance to the social changes now occurring in American society that its release to the public is important to public understanding of the changes themselves. We can also look forward to the collaboration of college teachers with paperback publishers in choosing new titles. There are many new ways in which teachers can anticipate reading needs in advance and cooperate with the publishers in making them available. Such projects as those of Joseph Loretan in the use of paperbacks in the New York schools are of great importance in improving education, since they make possible new modes of education directly relevant to this generation of children, modes which were never possible in the past and which show great promise for the future.

I would also suggest that there are great possiblities in the collaboration of television and film making with the paper-back publishers in order to take advantage of the wish of those who have been introduced, for example, to a poet of the stature of Robert Lowell through television, for copies of his poems. Television and films, dealing with poets or sculptors or poli-ticians or anyone else, can take advantage of the availability of paperbacks to develop curricula directly relevant to the tele-vision and film programs. New curriculum designs should seek directly the means through which this kind of coordination can be made more explicit. I thought, as I watched part of a television program about Robert Lowell last night, what an extraordinary advantage our young people have over the situa-tion we had when we were boys and girls; now one can be in the presence of the poet with a sharp sense of immediacy. The young people can hear not only the poems and see the poet, but can hear and see the critics of the poems, can see the plays acted, can gain a sense of the total character of the poet's work. A new richness is immediately introduced into the student's understanding of poetry itself. The extension of that experi-ence then becomes, quite naturally, the possession of the poet's books for further reading and enjoyment.

I conclude by suggesting that we need not only to make use of the new technologies in the speed of publication and the mass distribution of low-cost volumes, but that we also need to think of the revolution in mass culture as making possible a re-construction of contemporary experience. We need not think any longer in terms of a hierarchy of great works and those of lesser importance, since there is a kind of radical democracy on the drugstore rack where the *Iliad* stands beside *The Grapes of Wrath*. This is not to argue that one volume does not have a greater significance than another in the history of culture, or to deny that some books are greater than others. It is to say that, in the field of aesthetic experience, what may speak to one man at a given point of his life may not speak to another man. It is the aesthetic validity of the experience to which we must pay attention. We need to choose those works at those times in the lives of those persons who can then respond to the things we give them to read.

There is a familiar passage from Virginia Woolf which puts it beautifully. "Examine for a moment an ordinary mind on an ordinary day. The mind receives a myriad impression, trivial, fantastic, evanescent, or engraved with the sharpness of steel. From all sides they come, an incessant shower of innumerable atoms, and as they fall, as they shape themselves into the life of Monday or Tuesday, the accent falls differently from of old; the moment of importance came not here but there; so that, if the writer were a free man and not a slave, if he could write what he chose, not what he must, if he could base his work upon his own feeling and not upon convention, there would be no plot, no comedy, no tragedy, no love interest or catastrophe in the accepted style."

What Mrs. Woolf has told us in this passage is, I think, crucial to what we think about the mass culture and the high culture. The experience of the moment of an ordinary mind on an ordinary day is one through which the impressions form themselves according to predetermined patterns because each of us is himself. Each of us has his personal biography. But the patterns which emerge in our daily lives contain possibilities for fresh experiences, if only we can think of these patterns as open, if we can keep the daily flow of impressions free, without pre-instruction as to what we should be feeling and what we should be thinking.

It seems to me this is the deepest point of reference we can make in dealing with the revolution in reading which has been made available to us by the introduction of new publication methods under a new economic scheme. It gives us a chance to return to that unstructured acceptance of a whole variety of ideas, books, and writers, without which our lives become formed into patterns of banality.

Much for the Many

LELAND B. JACOBS
Professor of Education,
Teachers College, Columbia University

America is engaged in a great educational experiment, asking itself, "Can we educate in schools all of the children of all of the people?" There are, of course, many teachers and administrators, as well as great numbers of citizens not directly connected with school responsibilities, who think that this experiment is over—that as a people we have proved it can be done.

Actually, this great experiment is far from over. We still have many groups of children and youth not being served adequately to say we truly can educate all. Moreover, there is no great evidence of such unflagging support for education on the part of the populace as a whole and of strong pressure groups within this country to rest easy that free, well-balanced public education for all is assured. Nor do all educators consistently and whole-heartedly give themselves to the arduous task of making this great experiment an unqualified success.

There is considerable difference between ascertaining how many children are in school and how many are being well-educated. And, what is more, there are great differences as to what educators and laymen think it means to be "well-educated." Indeed, if one may be permitted to overgeneralize and to present extremes, there are today, basically, two strongly competing viewpoints as to how our children and youth will become "well-educated."

One of these competing viewpoints can be symbolized by the conveyor belt. Here, we put the child on a track (a fast track or a slow one; a track that develops a "custom model" or an ordinary one), and, while moving him along through school, we screw on certain "nuts and bolts" of skills, facts, and information. The nuts and bolts go through certain checks, based on the rote responses made to the technically systematized learning tasks. And, it is assumed, the child will come off the conveyor belt of schooling "well-educated" if the sequences of skills, facts, and information have been kept straight. He will be "well-educated" if those who have been putting on the nuts and bolts are clear about the content that everyone who passes through school should know. And the sooner, the faster, and the tighter the nuts and bolts can be put on the "model learner," the better.

The competing educational viewpoint holds that the task of the school in helping the child to become "well-educated" is to release the potential of the individual himself. Confront the child with "thinking-feeling" situations which provide him with opportunities to use what he knows; find out what he still needs to know and help him learn it. These educators presume that the child or youth is a dynamic human being. He has been given life but must make of that life what he can. He exists and he has potential.

To be "well-educated," according to this second viewpoint, is to use one's potential in a satisfying, socially constructive way.

Needless to say, my own sympathies are with this latter viewpoint. This releasing of the individual potentialities of all children and youth seems to me to be the way toward the realization of productive learnings on the part of the young. It seems to me, also, to be the direction that will encourage the development of those creative abilities and specialized talents that our country desperately needs, if it is to continue to be strong and vigorous.

Nobody here today would believe that there are productive children and unproductive ones, creative children and uncreative ones. We know that there are sparks of productivity and creativity in everyone. There are greater abilities, greater talents and lesser ones among the children and youth at school. But, rather than closed categorizations, what one deals with is a continuum of production and creation. Both the greater and the lesser abilities and talents should be equally served and nourished, and I submit that the way to such service and nourishment is through release of potential, rather than through prescription of a patent product.

This great experiment in attempting to educate all of the children of all of the people as well as the extreme stances just sketched cannot help but be influenced by the great surges in technology and automation which are upon us. If there are those who think that automation is still just around the corner, they are mistaken. With the stupendous technological "know-how" now in man's possession, automation has already, both physically and psychologically, made its impact on the life of our people in general, and on children in school in particular. Routine household chores require less time and energy from today's child, in his role as a member of the family. More leisure time is possible. Standardization, not only of work tasks but also of ways of living—what we sometimes call "the suburban mind" with its conformities and confinements, affects children's viewpoints, aspirations, behaviors. The introduction of technological tools of learning and mass media of communication into the classroom and the broader school life touch him in his values, his expectations of what schooling is, and his ways of coping with educational objectives. No one who would call himself a modern educator, of whichever persuasion alluded to earlier, would deny the impact of technology on today's pupils; nor would he subscribe to the opinion that automation is still some way off.

The great educational experiment must take technological advance into account as it continues to wrestle with the two central questions with which educators of all times have had to wrestle: What shall we teach? How shall we teach it?

These questions have to find their bearings in what seem essential ingredients of the American faith: the right of the individual to his fullest development; an interdependent group life; and the solution of problems through reasoned, reasonable, pragmatically workable ways and means. But, with the new realms of technology affecting the daily living, the great explosion of knowledge, and the faith in our way of life, the questions of what shall we teach our children and youth become increasingly complex. In the field now known as "the social studies," for example, shall we continue to teach geography, history, and civics, or some correlation or combination of these three? If so, what shall we do about economic education? Or about anthropology? In the "language arts," shall we teach grammar as a separate entity? If so, shall it be traditional grammar, transformational grammar, or yet some other proposal for knowing the features of a language?

In our times, however such questions as those just posed are resolved, schools will still have to provide children with significant confrontations in four major areas: idea content, skills content, aesthetic-feeling content, and social learnings. These are our central commitments on what to teach, as I see it. And we shall need to recognize that there are many ways of knowing; that one can know scientifically and one can know aesthetically; that one can know logically and intuitively. One can know through analysis and through synthesis. We shall need firmly to recognize the importance of many ways of knowing for all children and youth.

As, with balance in time, energies, attention, and materials, we guide children to appropriate idea content, skills content, aesthetic-feeling content, and social learnings, we must be sure that not one of them takes precedence over the others, that not one of these pivots is considered expendable.

And how shall we teach these contents? First with respect for the aloneness of each pupil. Each child, from the beginning of his living, "goes it alone," as a unique being. He has his own physical being, his own heartbeat, his own mentality, his own perceptions, values, aspirations. This is what I mean by aloneness. It should not be equated with loneliness, nor with differences. Rather, aloneness is the fact of making one's life into what that life can be, and in teaching it is the undergirding on which all other matters of method must be built.

Second, we should confront children with content that is in some way vital to the learner, that contributes to the making of the "common man" and to the expert individual. The kinds of confrontations with content that we pose and how we pose them —here is another key to how to teach. Does the confrontation encourage the child or youth to dig into the content being posed as educationally worthwhile? Whether a particular confrontation is posed as a topic, a problem, a key concept, an intriguing question, or the like, depends not on one's loyalty to a particular methodology so much as on the nature of the content inherent in the confrontation. And many ways of knowing will surely need to be brought to bear on the content being confronted if the experience is to lead toward helping the individual be "well-educated."

The way in which children are confronted with content directly affects their involvement, and involvement there must be, or else learning is superficial and lackadaisical. And the way in which children are confronted with content intended for the making of the "common man," or that which gives an individual what he should know to be one among others like him, will require teaching strategies that give the confrontation a universality of appeal, an urgency, and a social impact which can be recognized and accepted by all the children. On the other hand, those confrontations designed to lead children to the further fulfillment of their own individual expertness will be the ones that encourage more solitary pursuits, more leisurely attunements, more divergent outcomes. To be "well-educated," the individual will need the interplay of both these kinds of confrontations, with involvement in each contributing to what gives the young appropriate bases for his living well with others and his self-fulfillment, so far as his own chosen individual pursuits in knowing are concerned.

Nor can one overlook the enthusiasm of the teacher for the content being taught and the nature of the confrontations proposed in the curriculum. When a teacher is enthusiastic about the content and the materials provided for augmenting the confrontations with content, the child is more likely to be well taught. The teacher, then, will be at his best when he has considerable measure of freedom to style his teaching to use his best talents in the classroom. Imposed rigidities in methods and in choices of materials and the dictates, by closed systems, of sequences of teaching strategies are likely to dampen the good teacher's enthusiasm and thus rob children of the best that he has to give. If teacher enthusiasm is to be high, to the end that the child's involvement will be deep, conditions at school for both pupils and teachers must be such that a wholesome measure of freedom of operation is insured, rather than the imposition of closed, rote systematization of teaching procedures and learning tasks.

By now someone has been saying, "What in the world are you doing at a conference on paperback books? You haven't been talking about paperbacks at all."

On the contrary, I think I have. For whatever materials are used to help a child be "well-educated" must be appropriate to the curriculum and teaching commitments of the school system and of the individual teacher; they must be suitable to the potentialities of the children using them.

To be quite concrete, I think that one of the prime reasons for paperbacks in the school is that, through the use of them, the individualizing of instruction can be economically facilitated. I knew some teachers in rural schools forty years ago who used paperbacks to individualize practices: mail-order catalogs from Sears and Roebuck or Montgomery Ward. Today we can go much farther than that. With so many paperbacks available today, it is possible to have different kinds of reading material available at not too great cost, and any attempt at individualizing instruction is dependent on having extensive resources immediately at hand.

Another value of the paperbacks is that they are so economical that we can also have a selected library of beautiful, hardcover books, too. If we choose those areas in which the paperbacks serve just as well as the hardcover books have in the past, the money thus saved will make possible the opportunity for more children also to know the fine content in story, poetry, or informational writing made beautiful by the art of the illustrator and book designer. I feel that an important part of a child's or youth's education in the art of reading is to have experienced the joy of the feel of a magnificently made book in his own hands.

Then, too, through the use of paperbacks in the school, extended opportunities for critical thinking may be made possible. The less a person has to rely on what a single writer says, the greater the possibility that he will have to read critically. And surely in our country, a "well-educated" citizen is a critical reader—one who knows that no writer ever says everything there is to be said about anything. One who knows that, though a writer seems to be nowhere on the printed page, he is everywhere in what he writes. One who knows that the writer intends to get the reader to turn the page, to go on with him, to believe what he is saying. Paperbacks make it possible to bring into the classroom differing approaches, beliefs, judgments, viewpoints on the same subject. They encourage critical thinking by their very presence in the classroom, and this is something that reliance by all the children on a single instructional source does not and cannot make possible.

Through the use of paperbacks in schools, current knowledge and thinking and current art forms can be made available to children and youth immediately. Teachers will not have to wait for these materials to find their way into textbooks. The young are future-oriented. "Nowness" is tremendously important to them. The present-day world of thought and feeling can come into the classroom. The paperback can thus be a supplement, a complement, or a central instructional material for consideration of those manifestations of today's world of thought and action in elementary and secondary education.

In yet another way, paperbacks can serve classrooms well. Every dynamic teacher knows that in teaching there is an "et cetera" factor. The best-laid plans for teaching are in constant process of modification because it is not possible to anticipate all of the children's queries, concerns, or unexpected responses. Where vital teaching is going on, children's curiosities, concerns, and commitments are taken into account. Paperback books are a boon in this "et cetera" factor in instruction. Quickly, economically, and practically, the instructional materials previously not known to be needed can be supplied. Education does not have to be delayed or left dangling. Teaching plans can be modified because one can get the materials needed to make the modification reasonable and satisfying.

Paperback books can help immeasurably in augmenting the work of those teachers who want children not only to be able to read skillfully but also to turn to reading as a wonderful way to go on being "well-educated" throughout life. I have in my hands a hardcover book. Its title is *This Is Reading*. It is written by Frank Jennings. Let me read you one paragraph from it:

> Reading is a two-way process, between what someone writes, and what someone understands, and the sometimes awful difference between the two. It also involves what happens because of this understanding. The literary experience—for this kind of reading is that above all else—is one of the most profound, mind-shaping experiences in the life of man. It makes it possible for Plato and Christ to instruct us from thousands of years away. It joins minds and times together for the better management of our universe. It is as abstract as the idea of good. It is as precise and as practical as a door latch. It is the golden goad that makes man humane. It is this that we want our children to learn. For it is through the record that others leave to us in fact and fancy that we human beings live so richly in so short a time.[1]

Somehow these lines remind me of another favorite of mine— Alfred North Whitehead—who, in his *Aims of Education,* suggests three such aims: activity of thought, receptivity to beauty, and humane feelings. Since our country has seemed to put its faith in the common man and the fullest possible development of his potentialities through education, we who educate must take this faith seriously. Can we educate all the children of all the people? Can we help these children to be active in thought, receptive to beauty, embued with humane feelings?

How can the presently available paperbacks contribute best to this great experiment? What other paperbacks do we urgently need? Can the makers and publishers of paperbacks contribute to this great educational experiment even more than they are at the present time?

The great educational experiment is on. It has to succeed. It is our job to make it succeed. And as it does, it will be so because in classroom practices and procedures, in the confrontations with content, in the availability of instructional materials, there has been much for the many.

[1] Frank G. Jennings, *This Is Reading* (New York: Teachers College Press, Teachers College, Columbia University, 1965; second printing 1966), pp. 88–89.

Paperbacks Extend Reading Opportunities

C. TAYLOR WHITTIER
Superintendent of Schools,
Philadelphia, Pennsylvania

At a time when our conscience impels us to make universal education a reality, when our very survival rests on continuous advances in technology and in science, when knowledge is doubling so rapidly, and it's said that within an eight-year span, it will be doubled again, we are forced to become more and more narrow specialists if we are to probe further and further into the uncharted wilderness of new and growing knowledge. When one of our rival nations, just the other day, succeeded in accomplishing a soft landing on the moon, we recognize that we are truly in an era of growth and expansion and competition.

It is obvious that we cannot get away from one another by moving into or out of the city, or by building walls, or by digging holes, or even now by flying out into space. Thus, it seems to me that we should settle down to the business of learning to live together. And the business of living together means that we need to eradicate ignorance; that is the duty to which you and I have dedicated our professional lives. This means, I think, that we have to seek more effective ways to develop an understanding of our own cultural heritage, of the heritage of other people, of the differences which are apparent all around us, of the strengths of these differences, and that we need to develop techniques by which we can open new doors as substitutes for the personal experiences which many of our people have not had. And it is here, I think, that the outstanding opportunity for teachers rests—to bring to ever-increasing numbers of people—through vicarious experiences—opportunities to understand that which they have not personally had a chance to experience.

29

Actually, the problem is facing us of educating every child and every adult as well, and one of the things that we need to see if we can develop is illustrated by the statement in terms of building and understanding, while we are providing an education. It has been said that the typical American is a fellow who has just driven home from an Italian movie in his German car, is sitting on Danish furniture, drinking Brazilian coffee out of an English china cup, writing a letter on Irish linen paper, with a Japanese ball-point pen, complaining to his congressman about too much gold going overseas. In short, our job of education is still before us.

Some twenty-five years ago, a new concept was born in the world of literature. Its arrival was received with something less than enthusiasm in many publishing circles; the legitimacy of its birth was even questioned; and no one really was overly enthusiastic that it would ever mature into adulthood. Of course, I am talking about the paperback book.

But you may say, "Didn't paperbacks exist before then?"

This reminds me of an article by Lynne Poole which said that in the summer of 1860 a man named Erasmus Beagle in New York began publishing dime novels, which were small booklets, brightly colored in orange, brown, and green. In the course of the next five years, during the Civil War, he sold more than four million copies, and his best-seller was *Seth Jones,* a story of the New York wilderness of 1785. This book had sold more than half a million copies by 1865. It is quite true that, while many aspects of what you and I were seeing in the exhibit a few minutes ago certainly seemed to be new and bright and expanding, paperbacks have been with us for some time. As President Fischer mentioned, the paperback is not really in competition with other media of communication, but is a supplement and a tool that we need to learn to use ever more effectively. Back in 1939, a founder of Pocket Books, Inc., which began the more recent history of paperbacks, spent his early years in reprinting hardcover novels, particularly novels with emphasis on mystery, violence, and sex, which lent themselves to suggestive cover portraits. As Bennett Cerf, the witty president of Random House later remarked, "They were the kinds of books that had beautiful girls on the jackets, but no jackets on the beautiful girls." I can't help but say I couldn't find many of those jackets in the exhibit at this conference. Somebody censored this collection.

But the paperback field has become big business today. Total sales for 1964 have been placed at 315,000,000 books, 30,000 titles, costing $200,000,000. This represents approximately 11 per cent of the $1,800,000,000 book publishing industry in this country. All these figures, in themselves, are staggering, but the speed with which the modern-day paperbacks are being produced is perhaps even more staggering. I was interested to read recently, in *School Paperback Journal,* an article authored by Dr. Sidney Forman, Professor of Education and Librarian at Teachers College. The article said that recently developed machines are capable of producing and binding more than 18,000 copies an hour. This means 300 books every minute, or broken down still further, five books every second. That, no matter how you look at it, is a lot of books!

Dr. Forman also made another point that was surprising to me. In some areas of library service, the economics of printing paperbacks is making it possible to give them away at a cost less than the traditional practice of lending and retrieving hardcover books. I suppose this may be more true as the cost of hardcover books continues to go up, providing we can hold the prices of paperbacks down.

Two experiments, according to Dr. Forman, have proved this practice feasible. One was during the Second World War, when the government, between 1942 and 1946, purchased 1,324 titles in 123,000 paperbacks and distributed them to millions of persons who had never done reading before. The other example given was that the twenty-four dormitory-type libraries at the United States Military Academy at West Point were made up of selected paperbacks which substantially extended readership at a lower cost per unit than could be accomplished in the main library. Such is the extent of the economic impact of paperbacks on libraries, according to his report.

Another report, made at Syracuse University, suggests that the community colleges, while they are in the early stages of development, might well set up libraries of paperbacks. I think this would apply to many of the schools in the elementary and secondary fields as well. The catalog, *Paperbound Books in Print,* could serve the purpose of helping in the selection of titles in many of these areas which are so necessary as a part of our library collection process. It was pointed out that this could be an economic and speedy solution, to some extent at least, to the problems of dwindling and unavailable funds.

The growth of the paperback industry is by no means begrudged by the hardcover publishing companies. They have received more than $100,000,000 in royalties from paperbacks, and many of the companies have formed their own paperback affiliates. As the paperback book industry has grown steadily during the last quarter of a century, so has its stature. Some paperbacks of questionable taste are still with us, to be sure, and you can see these on the corner newsstands. But last year an estimated 40,000,000 copies were used in the nation's classrooms as textbooks and supplementary reading resources. Paperbacks, indeed, have made an impact on the education industry.

Leon Simpkins, president of Pocket Books, Inc., describes the rise in stature of paperbacks by twisting Gresham's Law a bit and applying it to the industry.

"Good books," he says, "are driving out the bad."

And these good books, applicable to both teachers and students, are rapidly multiplying. There are currently at least 4,000 titles suitable for use in various academic subjects, and some fifty new ones are being turned out each month. You can readily see in the exhibit collection that there are new ones constantly coming out. Although I must say that in our own city we do not use paperbacks as extensively as we would like, nevertheless they are being used to some extent and we are studying the feasibility of expanding their use.

Ideally, they are cheaper than hardcover resource material. But I think more important than the cost factor (and it is not entirely fair to evaluate the use of paperbacks on the matter of whether they are cheaper or not) is the ease in carrying them home and reading them. We have all discovered through experience that it is far easier to persuade our youngsters to read paperback books than to get them to read the same books in hard covers. One of the surveys among the New York City public schools showed that 75 per cent of over 2,500 students surveyed said they preferred a paperback to a harcover book.

"It's more fun to read. It's easier to read." And so on.

Smith College reports that, in some of the literature courses, students (perhaps thanks to paperbacks) are now reading eight to ten books per course when one book used to just about suffice in the pre-paperback era. Furthermore, it is estimated that half of the nation's public high schools and three-quarters of the private high schools now use paperbacks for coursework and/or supplementary reading. Of course, the advantages are obvious, and we won't go further into that at this time. Foremost in the minds of educators is that paperbacks actually encourage students to read. It is far easier for a student to pick up a paperback for 25, 50, or 95 cents—and I'll have to hasten to add that a considerably higher amount is true for the ones I just looked at—to take it home and read it at his own convenience.

Another boon to the field of education is that the availability of paperbacks to students greatly increases the range of our curricular offering. Our programs can be far more flexible and often considerably more interesting. It is one thing to read a few passages from, for example, Edgar Allan Poe, in a literature textbook, and quite another to digest Poe's works more deeply from a supplementary paperback book. There is also the opportunity of gaining access to many of the source materials that we digest sometimes in our collections to the detriment of developing a real understanding of the spirit and times in which the document originated.

There is also increasing interest by students in paperback course-outline series and instructional handbooks on what to expect and how to study for the College Board examinations, for example. And we must not forget the role of paperback dictionaries, not only for pupils and educators, but also for journalists, secretaries, and writers, in all other pursuits of communication throughout the world. There is a former professional journalist on our staff who informs me that the average reporter relies on his dictionary almost as heavily as a man of the cloth relies on his Bible.

He told us the story of the guided tour through the city room of one of our newspapers, in which the tour guide described the scene this way: "Over there on the right are the reporters. They can write, but they can't spell very well. Here in the center of the room are the editors. They can spell, but they can't write too well. And over there on the left is the sports department. Of course, they can't write or spell."

I'm afraid that more of our educators than would like to admit it face this spelling dilemma themselves in the whole process of teaching, and it's one we certainly haven't licked as yet. But with a handy, pocket-sized, paperback dictionary nearby, the problem at least gets into the realm of being able to be solved. It is no wonder, then, that the second largest-selling paperback in the twenty-five year history of the industry is the *Webster Pocket Dictionary,* with 14,000,000 copies sold. This brings to mind the question, of course, what is the all-time best-selling paperback book? And I would guess that some of you, like me, would find some difficulty in answering. What would you think it was? The evidence I have shows that it is the paperback edition of Dr. Benjamin Spock's book on baby and child care, which has sold 17,000,000 copies since its first publishing in 1946. Lest you might get carried away by the lofty reading levels of the American public, as symbolized by Dr. Spock and Mr. Webster, I found that number three on the paperback best-seller list, with 9,000,000 copies, was *Peyton Place,* which I suppose helps bear out the adage that variety is the spice of life.

But other lofty books are right up there among the leaders. At the five million mark, there is the University of Chicago's Spanish-English dictionary; then comes Roget's *Thesaurus.* Sandwiched in between these are some murder and mayhem epics by Mickey Spillane. Paperback books have also made inroads in the Parent-Teacher Associations. In many instances they're substituting paperback book sales for cake sales, and this may be not only good for learning, but good for our physical well-being as well. The associations simply order the paper-backs from the distributors and get their commission.

The impact of paperbacks extends not only to the students and to the PTA, but to the faculty as well. Each month more and more paperbacks debating the revolutionary and the con-troversial teaching profession are read avidly by teachers across the lands who themselves are swept up in the changing tide of technology in our education profession. These paperbacks deal with the vast new changes in curriculum, the crises facing public education today, as well as what the future holds for public education tomorrow. The availability of such material can only evoke interest to the professional educator, helping him to be-come more effective, more discerning and more sensitive to the problems revolving around him every day.

There is still another new field of education standing ready for the paperbacks—the field of helping to educate the vast numbers of disadvantaged pupils in our big cities across the nation. Such a program has been suggested by Vice President Hubert Humphrey. He has proposed a huge, free paperback book distribution program for underprivileged children as part of the federal government's War on Poverty. The project could be modeled after the government's free school-lunch program, Mr. Humphrey said, and I think it is an intriguing thought for all of us. If the Government can provide free food for hungry stomachs, he said, then it ought to be able to provide free food for hungry minds of youngsters who come from homes where there are no books, and very little stimulation. And I must say this is one of our great problems in education today. In Phila-delphia, as in every other large city across the land, we have many disadvantaged youngsters coming to school with no con-cept of reading or of color, or even of the names of the parts of their body, or what the world is like beyond the radius of a few blocks from their homes, which, incidentally, are run-down, bookless, and culturally barren. What a treasure just a little book might be for a boy or girl. It certainly would not teach him to read or to spell or to write, but it might actually ignite the critical spark of interest or motivation that means the dif-ference between a dropout and a high school graduate.

Speaking of difference, perhaps paperbacks also make a difference in many other corners of the world—whether people get to know about what the United States is really like or whether their view is distorted by much of the propaganda of alienation. How many of us realize that the United States Information Agency last year sent 11,000,000 paperbacks to forty different countries to promote a favorable picture of the United States abroad?

I think probably, after reviewing some of these statistics, you would agree with me that the paperback book has matured. The child of twenty-five years ago has come of age, and has, in fact, grown into a massive industry. Its influence extends into hundreds of thousands of the nation's classrooms, the nation's libraries, and the nation's home bookshelves for juveniles and adults alike. Its influence travels abroad into at least forty countries. Its impact has been dramatic. Its potential impact still remains to be felt. Its image is still marred at times by pornography, but this is inevitable and is true of some hardback books, and some motion pictures as well. However, this is a matter for the nation's conscience. It is an evidence of a maturing nation. And I trust that responsible Americans will reject this element of paperbacks and help to make Mr. Simpkins' theory of good books displacing bad a reality; indeed, it is already a reality in education. And I think that you and I welcome paperbacks and that they are here to stay, and that one of the problems that we face is how best to use these in educative process, in other words how to make them available.

I cannot resist at this time mentioning one of today's chuckles that illustrates the problem we face whenever we want to do something different from what our forefathers did. It is said that when our forefathers discovered this country, the Indians were running it. There were no taxes; there was no debt; the women did all the work. And our forefathers thought they could improve on a system like that. What I am getting at is that, as we are making these changes, we will have to give up some of the prerogatives and some of the ways in which we have operated in the past.

In looking over the scope of this conference, planned by the Committee of Forty, I am sure you have been impressed, as I have been, by the fact that paperbacks are here to stay, that they have already reached maturity in the eyes of many. And yet here is a challenge placed before all of us to see how we can make this maturity more effective. Throughout the conference there is an opportunity to delve deeper into the many details of one's interest, or to explore new areas, not just within one's own experience but perhaps an experience that we have not had a chance to delve into yet. For, while we are always seeking the new, we cannot overlook the past. The scope of this conference, if we look at the titles, is very impressive. We are going to have an opportunity to learn about teaching and learning as related to paperbacks, thinking, and reading, and, finally, how we make up paperback books. We are going to look at present practices, pilot projects, emerging developments, and new horizons—not only new horizons at different levels of education, but in various subjects. And to me it was interesting to note that we are planning to look at the use and effectiveness of paperbacks as they apply to the culturally deprived, or to the gifted, or to the slow, and I suppose in the slow is included the reluctant learner. Then, we have paperbacks for teachers for their professional growth, as well as for their use in the classroom. And then, of course, we have the old problems that we can't neglect to look at: how to select and administer the use of paperbacks; how textbooks will fit in as part of a multi-media approach to education, and how to handle book fairs and clubs. And, after we have looked so carefully at the wintertime use of books, there will be a special section for those interested in the summer use of books. Then, of course, no conference today would be in the social swim without a section dealing with federal programs—in relation to paperbacks, in this case.

So it seems to me that, as we look at the hopes and aspirations, as we look at the possibilities that lie before us, we can apply the learnings and the attitudes and the beliefs that we have had in our more traditional aspects of education. We should, then, approach with an open mind the possibilities of the more effective use of paperbacks, take off some of the shackles which have bound us (cost, for example), and make the paperback book an ever more effective tool. Regarding the future, we may hope to put more and more books into the hands of boys and girls who are really not benefiting much from education today, because here is the great challenge for the metropolitan areas. And this includes not only the city but the suburban areas where the bulk of our population will be residing.

Without understanding and without knowledge, and without breadth of perspective, we are not going to be able to make this an effective democracy. The very life blood of our nation today rests on how well you and I are able to use not only the paperback book, but other tools as well, so that we can have a balanced offering in curriculum, a balanced technique of presentation, realizing that there are many differences among our children and that there are many differences in the way that they learn.

I should like to close with a little poem about a dachshund—a dog for which I have strong personal feelings:

> There was a little Dachshund once
> So long he had no notion
> How long it took to notify
> His tail of his emotion.
>
> So while his little eyes were full
> Of present woe and sadness,
> His little tail kept wagging on
> Because of previous gladness.

And I am sure that, when we leave this conference after three days, we will carry with us many happy remembrances which will make our jobs more effective in that the spirit of the conference will extend far beyond the confines of this institution.

Teaching and Learning

HENRY M. BRICKELL
Associate Superintendent of Schools,
Manhasset, New York

Research tells us much more about learning than it does about teaching. Therefore, let us look at how people learn to see what it suggests about how we should teach.

Almost all of what I will say about learning comes from the informal papers of Ralph Tyler, the monographs of Percival Symonds and Goodwin Watson, the writings of Robert Gagne, the sixty-third yearbook of the National Society for the Study of Education, *Theories of Learning and Instruction,* edited by Ernest R. Hilgard, and the book, *Human Behavior,* by Bernard Berelsen and Gary Steiner. While I credit those men and countless other researchers for these ideas, I hasten to free them of blame for my rendition of the ideas.

One warning is in order: acquiring a motor skill is not the same as learning a concept; simple verbal learning is different from complex problem solving. Nevertheless, they are all lumped together here as if they followed the same patterns.

We begin with a definition: **To learn is to do something you have never done before (such as acting, thinking, or feeling) and to remember it so that you can do it again.**

1. *A person learns only the behavior which he himself produces.* In the words of that great Swiss psychologist, Jean Piaget, "The accent must be on auto-regulation, an active assimilation . . . the accent must be on the activity of the subject. Failing this there is no possible didactic or pedagogy which significantly transforms the subject." Or translating freely from the French: A child does not learn what the teacher does. He learns only what he does. How shall I emphasize this? Shall I simply evoke the memory of John Dewey on this hallowed ground? Or would you prefer references to research? If so, history, unfortunately, does not record the name of the experimental psychologist who first discovered that rats cannot learn to run mazes by hearing other rats explain how to do it. They must themselves run mazes. Perhaps I should simply remind you

that Socrates, a teacher who had a good bit worth saying, talked only half the time.

2. *New behavior must be satisfying if it is to be remembered.* A child must get some sort of satisfaction out of what he does if he is to remember it so that it can be reproduced at a later time. (Remember, incidentally, that it is "satisfying" to avoid punishment.) Much of the new behavior a person exhibits during his lifetime is *never* rewarded and is thus discarded. Much of his learned behavior is not *sufficiently* rewarded and is soon forgotten. In other words, the child has to do it himself and he has to like it. These two principles may be regarded as the cornerstones of teaching, the two great strategic problems of teaching being first, to arouse desirable behavior and second, to reward it so that it will persist.

3. *Old behavior must become dissatisfying if it is to be discarded.* When faced with a new problem a child will try to solve it with what he already knows. If the old method works, he is unlikely to learn anything new. But if the old method fails, the stage is set for learning.

4. *A person must know what new behavior he is to learn.* A child should know clearly what he is expected to do. Probably the most effective way to acquaint a child with what he is to learn is to demonstrate it. If the behavior is merely described, he will tend to learn the description rather than the behavior.

5. *The ideal learning goal is high but reachable with effort.* A goal which is too low can be reached with already-known behavior; thus no learning occurs. A goal which is too high cannot be reached even with reasonable effort; thus the new behavior fails, is not rewarded, and is not remembered.

6. *A person should set performance standards for himself.* In the best of circumstances, the learner sets a reasonable goal for himself, preferably competing with his own past record. There is probably no better way to assure his active engagement with the task and no better way to assure that the goal is high but reachable.

7. *A person learns through many senses—auditory, visual, kinesthetic, tactile.* A child can learn through watching, listening, smelling, touching, performing motions and so on. Some children learn given tasks best in certain ways, while others learn better in different ways. A good learning situation is rich with ways to learn through several senses.

8. *A learner should have at hand the materials needed for the new behavior.* If the desired behavior requires the sorting of facts, the solving of problems or the use of equipment, then the facts, problems or equipment must be present.

9. *The learner must receive information about the quality of his own performance.* A child must know how well he is doing in order

to know whether to continue his behavior or to reshape subsequent efforts in another direction.

10. *Time for practice is essential.* It takes time for a child to try out his new behavior, adding a bit, subtracting a bit, if he is to become effective, economical and speedy. Insufficient practice means incomplete learning and early forgetting.

11. *Succeeding repetitions of a new behavior should require slight modifications in it.* Sheer repetition becomes dull. As the behavior is called forth successively, the circumstances should contain some novel challenge which can be met only by modification of the behavior, preferably upward toward a more complex level of performance.

12. *Learning (like forgetting) proceeds rapidly at first, then more slowly. Periodic recall and practice at gradually increasing intervals are better than intensive practice followed by no practice.* A child learns most rapidly upon his first exposure to the new experience. But he almost immediately forgets much of what he has learned unless he practices it. The first practice should follow almost immediately upon the first learning, with successive practices scheduled at longer and longer intervals.

13. *Both learning and forgetting show "plateaus" in rate during which no change occurs.* A child is likely to pass through periods when he learns nothing new, despite continued efforts. Such plateaus, in both learning and forgetting, tend to be followed by spurts of change.

14. *Reward should follow the new behavior almost immediately and be clearly connected with it.* A small reward now works better than a big reward later. Neither one is effective unless the child knows exactly what he did to earn it.

15. *Satisfaction from the successful performance of the task is the best reward, but many other rewards can be substituted.* The simplest, most immediate and most appropriate source of satisfaction in learning is the gratification the child receives from doing the job successfully. This sort of reward fits the circumstances, is in perfect proportion to the size of the accomplishment, and is always available. However, a child will work for many other kinds of rewards, including those having nothing whatever to do with the learned task.

16. *Punishment is not the reverse of reward.* While a child's failure to earn satisfaction may be frustrating, he is usually willing to try again if success seems possible. Punishment, on the other hand, sets off a complex series of emotions which are usually disruptive to the specific learning situation and sometimes to a child's willingness to try other learning tasks.

17. *A person will learn behavior that is rewarded, whether or not*

that behavior is what the teacher intended to teach. A child will try to do the things which will gain him the greatest satisfaction. If the course has one set of objectives, but high grades or the teacher's admiration are given for a second set of behaviors, the child will try to learn the second set.

18. *A fresh, stimulating experience is rewarding in itself.* Children appear to seek novel experiences and often find satisfaction simply in undergoing an unusual experience, with no other reward offered or given.

19. *A person can learn many things at one time.* A child can draw many and diverse learnings from a single experience—including behaviors not necessarily intended, such as attitudes toward the subject, feelings about the teacher, knowledge of how to succeed in school and notions about his own worth and competence. Efficiently arranged learning experiences teach several desirable behaviors at once.

20. *General concepts are learned best through dealing with a large number of diverse illustrations.* A child gets the surest grasp of a principle by working with examples of it, having it formulated into a controlling idea, and then trying it out on new examples. This idea is not new. We may imagine that Jesus learned from some skillful old rabbi how to use a parable to make a principle unforgettable.

21. *Learning of general concepts sometimes occurs with a sudden flash of insight.* A child sometimes experiences the "Eureka!" or "Aha!" phenomenon, suddenly seeing a pattern of relationships without any apparent preliminary understanding of lesser principles, although usually he has advance familiarity with the detailed material underlying the concept. Learning acquired this way, it should be pointed out, does not fade out in the customary decelerating pattern, but tends to be retained over long periods.

22. *Learning transfers to other situations only to the degree that the situations are similar to the original and only to the degree that the skills and habits of transferring have been learned and practiced.* A child will not automatically transfer to a new situation what he has learned in other circumstances. He must be taught to seek and to recognize similarities in various situations and to apply his skills and knowledge to them. This is the law of learning we should most like to see repealed.

All of the above is true of the typical individual manner. These principles can be used to good effect by a tutor. But schools do not provide tutoring; they always ask teachers to deal with groups of children. Thus, certain other principles, of little interest to the tutor of a single child, become urgent for school teachers. The following are paramount:

23. *No two people make the identical response to any learning situation.* Children vary in their minds and personalities as much as in their appearance. Differences in heredity and in prior experiences create differences in intelligence, physical maturity, social skills, motor skills, attitudes, motives, drives, tastes, fears, and hopes. The result is that each child has a unique reaction to any given learning task.

24. *Individuals differ in rate and degree of learning and in rate and degree of forgetting.* Children may be considered "the same" only when they are equally ignorant of the matter to be learned. The moment teaching begins, the children become different. As teaching proceeds, the individual children become more and more and more different. It should, of course, be pointed out that *if* good materials are plentiful, *if* the teacher is truly superb, and *if* he works with energy and imagination, then the usual differences among the children become enormous. No one can teach so badly as to cause all children to learn anything at the same rate and to the same degree.

25. *Individuals grouped on any factor will range over several grade levels in other important factors.* Homogeneous grouping, except on a single factor, is impossible. Even then, the slightest amount of teaching will scatter the group in achievement. For practical purposes, children cannot be grouped in such a way that they can all be taught as if they were alike.

Very well, then. If this is what learning is like, what should teaching be like? In the few minutes remaining, let us take instructional materials—especially books—and merely illustrate what would happen if we seriously tried to make teaching match learning.

Individual Achievement Charts

The very beginning instructional material should be a wall chart—about four by six inches, I should say—listing in very fine print the specific behaviors the course offers to teach. (The chart would be of no use unless it named behaviors which a child could actually exhibit to the satisfaction of independent observers.) When the child arrived in September, his current achievement would be determined—that might take a week or two—and carefully plotted on the chart for him and the teacher to see.

There would be one of these charts on the wall for each child, spread all around the room. (An occasional child would hit the top or the bottom on everything. Either he would be sent on to another course, or the present one would have to be expanded to fit him.) As teaching commenced, the child's progress would be plotted on the chart regularly, say once every period in high schools and about seven times a day in elementary schools. No doubt it would make an extremely jagged line. About once a month the chart would come off the wall and be sent home with the child—his report card for his mother and dad, of course. They could examine his status and his growth since September. And for the very first time they would know what he could do rather than being told that he could perform exactly 83 per cent of some undescribed body of behavior called English 10.

If the four-by-six-inch size proved inconvenient by restricting light or ventilation, the charts could perhaps be reduced to booklet form—but only if *all* of them could somehow be kept constantly in view of the teacher and *each* of them constantly in view of the child whose learning it recorded. That is of utmost importance.

Variation of Materials

Next, we need materials designed to teach all of the behaviors on the chart. The same ideas and information ought to be represented in several symbolic forms. A child should be able to read about, listen to, see pictures of, hold in his hands, watch performed and, of course, act out himself the things to be learned. If an idea can best be expressed in a motion picture, it should be. But it should also be represented in still pictures, in music, in printed words and in physical objects so that the child can sense it in several ways.

The teacher will have to have all of the materials constantly at hand since those jagged lines on the charts will never arrive at the same point simultaneously. It will not do to have Charlotte read next April the two-page explanation she needed last October.

Graduated but Ungraded

It is only the schools which are graded; learning has never been graded. Accordingly, all instructional materials should be ungraded. That is, all grade identification should be totally removed—and I *don't* mean cleverly coded for the teacher's private use. When the teacher picks up the ungraded material and asks, "Who is this for?" someone ought to be nearby to say something like this:

See this device right here? If you will use it as directed with the child, you can determine his present performance level and also his capacity and his readiness for the next step in learning what that particular instructional material you have in your hand is designed to teach. Now if he performs in the lower range right about here, he is not ready for that material you are holding, and he ought to start with the next lower level. If he performs in here somewhere, look more closely and you will see *where* he should start in your material. Of course, if he should perform in this range up here, he already knows what that material is designed to teach and he should move to the next higher level. And, by the way—if you have another child to teach, you will want to repeat the whole process with him, too.

If you tried to picture what instructional material that teacher was holding as I spoke, I hope some of you were thinking of spelling books and others of sheet music for the clarinet, or of a programmed textbook in algebra, or a filmstrip on reproduction in fruit flies, or tape-recorded pattern drills in Portuguese, or a video tape of our latest moon shot, or a textbook on economics, or blocks in assorted geometric shapes. I had all those in mind. As I said, none should have grade levels stamped on them. Note, however, that all can be assigned a place in a graduated sequence. The teacher must then be helped to find where the child is in that sequence.

Reading on Many Levels

A textbook, as we all know, is actually a syllabus—a course of study—filled in with enough words and pictures for the student to make his way through it in about nine months with a good bit of help from the teacher. Since there is no prospect of finding thirty or forty children able to learn the same thing at the same time, no teacher would ever think of ordering thirty or forty copies of the same textbook. At first I was going to suggest that you borrow the school paper cutter and convert all the textbooks into short monographs to be handed out as pupils needed them. But of course this is not practical because the teaching materials for taking one child through a syllabus cannot be the same as the teaching materials for taking another child through it. Thus, you never need thirty or forty copies of identical pupil reading material.

On the other hand you might need three copies of a book written at about the level of *Reader's Digest,* five copies of another book on the same topic written in the language of the *Saturday Evening Post,* twelve written at the level of *Time Magazine,* four at the level of *Atlantic,* and one in the language of *Scientific American.* Thus equipped, you could have one or several students learning the same topic simultaneously but with materials suited to them.

Self-Instructional Materials

All materials should be self-instructional insofar as possible. The student should be able to engage himself actively and successfully with the material in the absence of a teacher. No materials should be designed so that the student is deliberately brought to an abrupt halt and sent to the teacher for help in jumping a hurdle. Many of today's textbooks and almost all workbooks assume regular classroom learning as a prerequisite to their use. The workbook, for example, does not offer initial teaching, but only practice of what has already been learned. The student is not able to move through it without help. Such a tool is well-suited to the purpose of mass instruction. It is especially useful for making fast students wait at the gate until slow ones catch up. Many teachers use workbooks for precisely this purpose.

Illustrating General Principles

Illustrations of general principles ought to be lavish in quantity and rich in quality. The materials ought to create comprehensive pictures of prototype situations. They ought to suggest the reality of the situation wherever possible. A social studies teacher should be able to dump onto the table a box full of letters, newspaper clippings, recorded telephone conversations, photographs, a motion picture of an event as seen through the eyes of a single witness and other such material, so that he can say to three able students: "Each of you write the history of the event described in this box. You have read history, you have studied the criteria of good historiography—now go write some. Then we can see how much 'history' is in the event, how much in the historian."

The same teacher ought to be able to dump out a corroded metal band, a fragment of a clay pot, a piece of fabric, a piece of jewelry with human figures on it, a photograph of a cornice, and say to a student, "These were excavated along the Nile about 150 miles south of Cairo during the building of the Aswan Dam. See what you can figure out about the people who left them behind."

Or he should be able to hand a student a sheaf of one nation's government reports filled with tables of economic data and ask for an analysis of trends in the productivity of that nation during the past decade.

Making Individualized Teaching Possible

Let me conclude with a personal experience. Not long ago I joined a team of school visitors who were searching through classes with fewer than twenty pupils in wealthy New York suburbs, looking in these enriched settings for harbingers of the

School of 1980, which we presumed would take seriously the principles of learning outlined above and would accordingly devote itself to individual instruction. During my own visits to these small classes in well-supported schools, which we hoped might already show in the early 1960's what would become universal in the 1980's, I used a simple rule of thumb upon entering the classroom: Were all the children doing the same thing at the same time? If so, I would close the door and move on.

When the team gathered afterwards to search its observations for generalizations, it reported some examples of individualized teaching. We had found it in kindergartens and sometimes in first and second grade, but we noted that it became rarer in successively higher grades—except in art rooms at all grade levels, where it took the worst imaginable teaching to crush it out, and in industrial art shops, in home economics rooms, in instrumental music groups, in bookkeeping classes, and in a few other places. It was notably absent in the "academic" subjects—English, social studies, mathematics, science, and foreign languages —except in the teaching of reading, where we found individualized instruction at almost all grade levels, and in the teaching of science in the occasional well-equipped laboratory.

What struck me most forcibly, and I was not prepared for it, was the fact that we almost never found individual instruction *except in the presence of ample space and ample teaching materials.* Space and materials—room for the child to do something besides sit and things for him to pay attention to besides the teacher's voice.

A lot of those things had paper backs.

Paperbacks in New York City

JOSEPH O. LORETAN

*Deputy Superintendent of Schools,
Instruction and Curriculum
Board of Education of the City of New York*

We in New York City have been having an adventure with paperback books. Our paperbacks are tied in with an educational reform and curriculum revision movement, and not having the paperbacks would have slowed us up considerably. I would divide our activities into material—paperback material —that we have been looking at, and material that we have been creating. I want to talk a little bit about the paperback material that we have been creating in connection with our program of human relations. I think that you will be fascinated with this story. I plan to talk a little bit about the research work that we have done in connection with paperbacks later on. There are four of these paperbacks that we created. They cost 33 cents apiece, and I am not selling them! They are put out by Silver Burdett.

My assistant, Mrs. Shelley Umans, and I sat down and dreamed up a project that would get books into the hands of the youngsters in New York City—a project based on the following question: Are there people now living in the ghettos in New York City, people who were born and/or raised there, who have become important people in the community? Now, I think you can guess why we selected this idea. We have in the many New York City communities thousands and thousands of young people who think that if they were raised in this kind of a situation they have nowhere to go, they are not going to make it, they might just as well give up any ideals, they might just as well not try.

We set up a committee, a task force, to help us find people with great community insight, to help us in a very quiet way to discover heroes, and we call them heroes. As the editor said, "They may not be slaying dragons and they may not be on fiery steeds, charging against the enemy, but they are part of the folk-lore of a great city and they are doing something that is enormously significant for us. They are giving youngsters the concept that people in the situation that I find myself in—speaking for a boy or a girl—can make it, because people *have* made it." We are going to saturate the schools with this material. We want to give it to the youngsters. And we are going to make money on this, just as we are with another type of paperback, the "Building Reading Power" series, which we sold to Charles E. Merrill Books, Inc., to produce. Our schools get a discount on these books and we get royalties. Yesterday we got a check for $2,500, small in a big city budget, but it does indicate that there are challenges that we school people can accept and that there are people in the commercial and business world who like imagination and who can work with us. This is a flexible opportunity that we thought we could not miss.

Now, we have another problem in the big city—and this is a problem all over the nation—perhaps even more of a problem in the rest of the nation than in New York. That is the abysmal ignorance of people about the assets, the contributions, and the material wealth that have been produced by the so-called minority groups. I would not want to hurt the feelings of this fine audience, but I suspect that most of you, or most of us I should say, have only a dim, fuzzy idea of the contributions of the Irish, of the Negro, or of the Latin-Americans to our culture. We first decided to circulate reference books of good substantial size, and we did, but, when we wanted to put out a couple of hundred thousand copies of a publication quickly, we proceeded again to produce our own paperbacks. We put out three paperbacks for teachers: *The Negro in American History, Puerto Rican Profiles,* and *Dante: A Representative of Italian Culture.* I shall comment on these further at a later point.

We also developed a brand new course of study in science, but nobody was ready with pupil materials. Not one of the available textbooks was useful to us. So, we worked out a plan with a textbook company to produce attractive, pocket-size, science material called *The Materials of Life.*

We gained about two years and created a small revolution in

science teaching by being able to give this book to every single youngster. He read it and he kept it. It was his. We are encouraging the school principals to give paperback books to students so that, with a reasonably small amount of money, we can help create personal libraries for the youngsters all around our city.

Finally, in this vein, I would like to describe the most recent paperback project in which members of the New York City School System have been involved. It is a packet of about ten paperbacks, produced by Educational Services Incorporated as the basis for a new approach to teaching history and the social sciences. The materials are designed to help youngsters become their own historians, to help them understand the concept of the historian and how history is written. Here in this one packet, we have a short description of the New England plantations, a copy of an original document, a short and true description of the commodities and discommodities of that part of the country, a description, a kind of promotion scheme that was presented for the person that they were trying to encourage to come to America. My comment on this is that here we have a dozen items in which the youngster, using original source material, begins to create and understand some of the concepts we are trying to put across in the question, "How do you understand history today and tomorrow?" And we answer that question by saying you make a good, deep, powerful, thorough study of one or two of the epochs or periods, and you fit this into a setting in which the rest of history and geography and economics and the whole gamut of the disciplines that make up the social sciences can be drawn out, built, and used in the schools.

We are happy in the creation of these materials and in joining with others in doing it. It used to take, I suppose, from two to four years to put out a solid, responsibly written textbook. We in New York have major curriculum revisions going on in at least four areas—mathematics, science, English, and the social sciences, and we think that, by using the paperback material adroitly, we can gain probably two years or three years in terms of a head start, in terms of a changeover in the instructional pattern and in curriculum revision. I suspect what will contain the heart or the essence of the narrative of history, the narrative of the critical element in literature and composition, and the critical elements in science, and that the paperbacks will become satellite materials. I will be recommending to the Board of Education in New York City a plan in which most of these paperbacks, at least some each year, will be given to the youngsters.

Now, there are some problems. I think one of the basic problems is that the paperbacks are in danger of pricing themselves out of the market, especially the so-called slick-covered ones. They cost too much. We have been making comparative studies.

Now, I would like to describe some of our plans in New York City and then comment upon some of the recommendations made by a research group that has been assaying the value of paperbacks in the schools. As we list our textbooks in the next listing period, we shall put down the name of a hardcover book in literature, history, science, mathematics, for example. Then we will put the price of the book right next to this listing. We can then probably list the related paperback books with just the change of a letter—"T" for the textbook list and "P" for the paperback list. Thus, the paperbacks will be listed and priced right next to the hardcover books. We shall do this for the paperback industry because we think, every once in a while, that they are getting rich too fast. If we list the prices of the paperbacks next to the hardcover books, and people see that sometimes the difference is only 30 or 40 cents, they will buy the hardcover books because they last longer. I don't want to overemphasize durability or lack of durability; I merely want to point out to this fine, new industry that it is going to price itself out of the market rather quickly if the upward trend of the cost of paperbacks continues at its present—in my estimation—alarming rate.

The next area in which we feel we are helping teachers to use this new and flexible medium is that of teacher training. In the last year and a half, we have put out in quick succession three "thought" books. The first is *The Negro in American History;* the book is directed mainly toward teachers, but it is also available to students in the junior and senior high schools. Not much had been written about the Negro in American history until we put this book out, and the book has become something of a standard for all book publishers. It is an authentic volume. Several of the best scholars in the nation worked on it. This is an outstanding piece of work in which we tried not so much to change teachers' attitudes as to give them information that was crucial to their understanding—information that simply did not appear in any of the existing teaching textbooks. Yet, within a few months we were able to put out a production which has been enormously useful.

We followed our Negro history with a true-life story of the Puerto Ricans, *Puerto Rican Profiles*; this book concerns a Latin-American group about which little or nothing has been told. And, very recently, we finished our latest production, *Dante*. Since 1965 was the seven hundredth anniversary of Dante's birth, we instituted a three-month study on his life and then published the results for use of the teachers. This sort of publishing—answering a special need quickly—seems to be an avenue in which paperbacks have a wonderful future.

Now I would like to talk about some recommendations made on the basis of a research study that included all of the high schools and some of the junior high schools in New York City. Approximately a hundred schools took part. The study involved the chairmen of English departments, and what resulted were five recommendations, the essence of which I shall offer for your consideration.

Recommendation number one is that literary works in paper-back form for regular use in high school English classes be purchased with Board of Education funds at the direction of the principal and the department chairman. In New York this has been enormously helpful in putting literary works in their full, unabridged forms into the hands of youngsters. This is the job which, up until now, has been done by the anthologies. However, an anthology presents only tiny bits of an author, whereas, now—for practically the same cost—the youngsters can have a dozen authors in unabridged form and can achieve the sense of excitement that comes from reading the original work.

The second recommendation is that special efforts be made to supply such paperbacks to the youngsters in the so-called disadvantaged areas, since these are the ones who will derive the greatest benefit out of having them. The more gifted students already have these books in their homes, because either they or their parents have been sufficiently motivated to acquire them. Thus, the books the chairmen felt were the most useful were those that went to the disadvantaged youngsters.

Recommendation number three is that the introduction of paperbacks into the English Department should involve all teachers, and you can see the reason for that. Any teacher preparing to use a paperback, lacking teaching aids, must undertake to supply substitutes, and of course, the way that was done was to furnish the teaching aid. We put out little publication which consisted entirely of suggestions for teachers made in relation to the problems that they might have.

Recommendation number four stated that the departments initiating the use of paperbacks should consider whether mass-market or quality editions best fit their needs. Mass-market textbooks demand lower expenditures and hence, are appropriate for meeting a temporary need—for example, supplementing a store of hardcover textbooks, trying out titles for a broadened curriculum and for meeting individual needs, or providing material for an experimental purpose. If it is foreseen that a title will be used indefinitely and that, therefore, the books will be rotated as are hardcover textbooks, then fine-quality paperbacks may be advisable. Their greater durability would offset their higher initial cost. We subjected hardcover books and the quality paperbacks to consistent use in a number of different schools, and we found very little difference in durability. No one has come up with final, ultimate, definitive results on durability tests in every kind of school. In some schools, the paperbacks and the hardcover textbooks lasted about the same length of time; in other schools the hardcover books took worse beatings than the paperbacks did. So no one at this stage can offer a final and ultimate conclusion as to the strength and durability of these different books. However, the recommendation seems a sensible one. Here we have a new, important tool that can be used by the principal of the school and by the teachers on the basis of need. Perhaps a new course is to be introduced, or some experimental work is to be tried out. Instead of having to wait for and bear the expense of creating a hardcover book, we can invent or help create a paperback that will serve the purpose.

Parents and youngsters did not take a stand on the matter of durability. In effect, they said, "We just like to have the paperbacks, and we're not concerned about your durability study." I suppose such an attitude is representative of our affluent society. Everything is packaged, everything is wrapped, and the people are accustomed to the paperback approach.

The fifth and last recommendation is one that, of course, we all agree on. It is that the study of the paperback textbook be continued. Now, my big argument, and one that I am pursuing with the Board of Education, is that, insofar as is possible, paperbacks should be given outright to the youngsters. In the long range, what we are hoping is that society will upgrade itself. If we school people are going to uplift, if we are going to raise the standards and values of the total community, we will not do it as efficiently with a loan system. The loan system, whether it involves library books or textbooks, goes back to the scarcity philosophy that was based on the time when books were written by hand, on parchment or papyrus, when Bibles were carefully chained to the altars in the churches and monasteries. I suggest that, for the future, the concept of a librarian as a custodian of books is as dated as the dinosaur, that what we need instead of custodians of books are flexible ways of getting many, many more people to own them, to read them, to use them in every conceivable way. There is an ingenious librarian in White Plains who has been using a trick that may not be new to many of you. She has an enormous shelf of paperbacks bearing a sign that says, "Borrow them and return them," but there is no card stamping and no reporting of the books being taken out. I have seen youngsters going out with their hands full of them, but the librarian says that 99 per cent of them come back. In addition, she says, the students themselves frequently contribute other books that they have found interesting. They say, "Look, let me give you this one. This is a wonderful one."

I should like to close with an incident told to me by one of my staff members who went into a church near the New York City

Board of Education to do a kind and friendly act, not really an act of devotion. But in the back of the church there was an enormous display of paperback books. And as my staff member was going along—you know how we school people are forever stealing things—she was looking at these books and certainly seemingly being tempted. So she said to a young curate: "I don't see any prices on these books. I don't see any guards here." And he answered, "Oh, we'd like it if they were taken by people!" I think this anecdote provides an object lesson for the school community: let's make sure the kids get as many books as possible and gamble that they will be used. This is where budgets need to be changed. With the federal funds now available it should be possible for us to change our psychology and to simply encourage as much reading as we can, without worrying about whether the books get returned. What is needed is a new philosophy, a philosophy in which the teachers, the principals, and the school board members are interested in improving the culture, the educational climate in the community. I think school boards should be interested in giving youngsters books.

There was a revolution in education, you may remember, in which we supposedly achieved the ideal of free books for youngsters, but we really do not have free books for youngsters. We have books that we lend them for a little while, and, as soon as they get interested in them and dig into them, we take them back. We are Indian givers. I think we in the educational community ought to change our philosophy and pursue the idea of giving youngsters as many books as possible, making them attractive, making them useful, and in that way improving the culture of the community.

Paperback Books in New Jersey

MAX BOGART
Assistant Director,
Division of Curriculum and Instruction
New Jersey State Education Department

According to the *Handbook of Research on Teaching,* ". . . research on reading instruction comprises more material than does research in any other part of the curriculum." In 1960, W. S. Gray estimated that "some 4,000 careful scientific studies on the teaching of reading are available," and he added that "other interpretive and descriptive writing on this subject would at least double this number of reports." If we add the hundreds of research pieces completed during the past five years, the total figure must be a staggering one. And we would probably think that most reading problems had been covered to some degree by some phase of research. However, it is interesting that on many occasions the desired research material is unavailable. A major reason for our recent study in New Jersey was to find answers to certain questions.

Within the last few years, much has been written and said about the paperback book revolution and about the paperback book being "firmly rooted" in American cultural life. We know that the sales of paperback books are impressive. As the speaker here yesterday pointed out, about 300,000,000 sales a year. We know that millions of children and youth are buying and reading all kinds of paperback books, especially out of school.

In recent years many writers have claimed that these books have created a powerful impact on the curriculum of high schools and colleges. Undoubtedly the number of schools using these books as an integral part of the curriculum have multiplied, but data on the effects of increased utilization have been meager. Except for isolated classroom experiences, we knew very little in terms of the effects of paperbound books on the teaching and learning process.

Several years ago, a thorough analysis of the existing reports indicated that interested persons had been playing hunches, relying almost entirely on personal and limited experience in their individual classrooms. Now, honest as such notions may be, they still remain intuitive, lacking verification. But have you ever tried to sell a paperback program to a school board without sufficient data to support your sales pitch? Have you ever faced a board composed of scientists, trained in analysis of facts, or a board of practical business men, who want to know what such an innovation will cost, as compared with the hardcover textbook now in use? Or have you confronted reluctant teachers and school administrators, who are very often hostile to any change in current practices? You may recall Mark Twain's words, "Nothing needs reform as much as other people's habits."

As I visited schools in New Jersey and other states, I urged teachers to cast away the five-pound anthology and the so-called basal reader as a first step in vitalizing or revitalizing the English curriculum. I suggested that a paperback book program, stressing individualized reading, be substituted to combat the dull, mechanical, threadbare, and—yes—often sterile materials now in wide use. Invariably, the questions of cost and durability would arise, and, lacking the pertinent data, I would counter arguments about enrichment and improved educational outcomes. But my appeal was not factual. Therefore, to persuade the schools, we embarked on an investigation of the durability of paperback books. As we studied the total problem, however, we concluded that this should be only one aspect of the proposed project.

The general purpose of the study was a systematic analysis of the effects of trade paperback books upon the English language arts curriculum of the public elementary and secondary schools in our state. Answers were sought to the following questions:

1. At which grade levels have paperback books affected curriculum?

2. How early in the elementary school may paperbacks be used extensively?

3. To what extent are available paperback books adequate as compared with basal readers and early reading textbooks?

4. What proportionate use is made of paperbacks as classroom textbooks, as supplementary assignments, and as library reading?

5. How effective are paperback books in the development of reading habits and skills?

6. Where paperback books are used, what changes are evident in learning and in teacher and student attitudes?

7. How durable are paperback books?

The American Book Publishers Council was approached to ascertain their interest in such a study. Forty-five publishers indicated that they were willing to participate on an individual basis. They distributed over forty thousand books to the participating schools without charge, the schools making all decisions concerning titles and editions. The American Book Publishers Council exerted no control whatsoever over the policies, the procedures, or the final evaluation of the project. The study was financed by a grant from the New World Foundation, and a matching sum from our own New Jersey State Department of Education.

Fifty elementary and secondary schools were selected according to geographical location with a minimum of one school from each of the twenty-one counties of the state. We wanted representation from all grade levels—one through twelve—and various sized schools to insure varied types of programs. We made a socioeconomic profile of each community to insure a cross-section sampling; thus our schools were identified as lower-class, middle-class, and upper-class. We also made up a cross-section in terms of the type and size of communities, to insure representation of rural, suburban, and city schools. The final criterion was the willingness of the teachers and the administrators to participate. We felt that, if these people were really not enthusiastic about this innovation, not much could be accomplished. A total of 8,377 students were involved in the study.

Eric Goldman, who teaches history at Princeton University, wrote a few years ago: "Every so often it happened. The world would be rushing along, exalting and denouncing, and suddenly somebody, somewhere, facing a stack of blank paper, would touch the paper with magic. A book appeared and things were never quite the same."

In analyzing the results of this study, one may readily conclude that paperbacks are a kind of magic. It would be absurd to claim that they represent a panacea, a cure-all to cure all. But from the moment these books appeared in these classrooms, and from the moment these 8,377 students came into contact with them, things have never been the same in these fifty elementary and secondary schools. Here are some of the highlights from the data, compiled from the student, teacher, and administrator questionnaires, from teacher logs which were kept on a weekly basis, from the many interviews that members of our staff had with the teachers, the students, and the school administrators, and from hundreds and hundreds of narrative reports received from these sources.

It was found that the existence and use of a variety of trade paperback books, easily accessible in the classroom, effected desirable changes in most students. A majority of the students, about 58 per cent, indicated that their general interest in reading was greater than ever before; about 68 per cent believed that all their school work—beyond the English program—had improved; and about 23 per cent felt the level of improvement was considerable in all subjects, although the books used were only in the English curriculum. About 46 per cent found schoolwork more challenging in all subjects as a result of the contact with these books, and some 69 per cent thought schoolwork was now more interesting.

The reports indicated that these youngsters, both the children in the elementary schools and the young people in the secondary schools, were now talking more than ever about books in class discussions and with their friends outside of school. Some of them indicated that they were now talking to their teachers for the first time about books.

The study disclosed that reluctant readers are not quite so reluctant when they participate in a program that supplies appropriate books for their particular levels of interest. Many slow learners and many culturally disadvantaged students read whole books for the first time and reported that they enjoyed this experience. As for the academically talented and the gifted youngsters, they found these books exceedingly challenging. They had to probe in depth for the first time, and many of them responded with enthusiasm. (This word "enthusiasm" comes up in a number of places in our report. It is very difficult to measure enthusiasm, yet the youngsters told us over and over again how enthusiastic they were about the paperback books.)

Generally, most students reported that they were devoting more leisure time to reading and that their interests broadened as a result of this extension beyond the required textbook in school. We found that more positive attitudes toward learning developed on a schoolwide basis. Improvement was noted by the English teachers in the writing and speaking components of the English language arts curriculum, and many students reported that they now started personal libraries. An interesting and I think meaningful by-product of the project was the information from both elementary and secondary schools that the parents, the brothers and sisters of the participating students were borrowing these books that were brought home and they, in turn, were also reading more than before.

Students from the first grade through the senior year in high school reported that they were attracted to the paperback books because of the variety of subject matter, the convenient size, and the colorful artistic covers—and you can't minimize this. They were fascinated by these covers that the paperback book publishers have produced. Voluntary selection of books was another important response. The students were no longer being given the book to read, but, rather, they were given a choice of what to read for the following day or the following week. The data, in short, revealed that this project shaped or reshaped the habit of reading by generating a hunger for books.

As for the teachers' reactions, more than 82 per cent of those involved reported that their views had changed regarding approaches to reading. Many stated that they now favored a thematic unit approach. Over 85 per cent said their teaching methods had changed; and about 75 per cent reported that curriculum changes were planned or in progress with the emphasis on more individualized reading and the initiation, continuation or the expansion of classroom libraries. The reasons noted by the teachers for these changes were the greater variety and flexibility afforded by paperback books, the modification in both student and teacher attitudes toward reading, and, last but not least, the cost factor. Incidentally, the changes in student attitudes reported by the teachers were remarkably similar to the reports made by the students themselves.

It should be noted that many teachers lacked information about appropriate books for specific grade levels. As a result of this project, many of the teachers became more familiar with book lists and with library resources. Perhaps the most negative and depressing aspects of the study were the revelations that many teachers were unfamilair with paperback editions and with library reference materials which provide such information. Unhappily, the study disclosed that, beyond the required textbook assignments, many teachers themselves were nonreaders. How can nonreaders instill a love of and necessity for reading? How will they develop and nurture the lifetime reading habit?

The *New York Times* of February 23, 1964, quoted Lord McCorquodale: "I sometimes think that educationists are so accustomed to instructing young people that they forget it is possible to be instructed themselves."

Another negative point of interest was the rigidity of book selection and assignment by many teachers. It was as if a given title were fixed, or frozen, or decreed for a specific grade level. You may remember the French adage, "The more things change, the more they remain the same." Despite the freedom of selection, many teachers chose the same titles and the same authors that they had been using before, only thinking now that if they were in the soft covers something would happen in the classroom. They failed to recognize that the paperback book program has freed them from any conventional or traditional kind of curriculum pattern. Repeatedly it was found that, where the "old chestnuts" were used almost exclusively, little or no change was seen, either in the students' attitudes or in their reading habits. The paperback book by itself could not overcome this sort of academic obstacle.

As for the school administrators, some 72 per cent stated that the project had a marked effect on the entire school program. In fact, over 52 per cent were planning, or had already started significant curriculum changes as a result of this project.

What about the durability of paperback books? A majority of the teachers, about 53 per cent, found it was possible to get four to ten readings from a single book. A substantial number, 36 per cent, used the books for more than ten readings. Obviously, the number of readings varied according to the grade level, the school location, the reading and book-care habits of the individual students, and the specific edition. About 67 per cent of the teachers estimated that more than 75 per cent of the books in the project could be used the following year. It was concluded that, under "normal conditions," a paperback book collection can serve a classroom for two or more years.

What are some of the implications that can be drawn from this study? Through an extensive paperback book program, the elementary and secondary schools can gain greater curriculum flexibility and make use of a variety of instructional approaches. We can now begin to teach courses whose content will be current because of the very up-to-date nature of the materials. We can provide many opportunities for more creative and effective instruction with emphasis on experimentation. Next, we can stimulate and enlarge the reading interests of most students and improve the development of reading skills.

Another implication is that we can change attitudes toward learning and toward school. Based on the objective data and on the student narrative responses—such as the repeated assertion of high school seniors that this paperback book project was the most stimulating and exciting experience in their entire academic life from kindergarten through the twelfth grade, we may assume that there will be some kind of carry-over affecting many phases of school activity.

The study concludes with some twenty recommendations, eleven of which follow, that can be supported by the findings:

1. Classrooms—elementary and secondary—should contain extensive paperback book collections.
2. Individualized reading programs should be expanded with the paperback book as the core of that program.
3. Free reading should not be graded because grades can hinder enjoyment.
4. There ought to be an increase in the number of paperback book fairs and book stores, and these should be established wherever feasible to encourage students to build their own personal libraries.
5. Local merchants should be encouraged to stock recommended paperback books, and school people ought to tell their local merchants what books they want in their stores.
6. Central libraries should make greater use of these paperback books.
7. School budgets should be flexible enough to allow teachers to order paperback books when and as they are needed.
8. Reading, or literature, should not be isolated from other components of the English language arts curriculum.
9. Colleges of education should help teachers-in-training to understand the consequences of the paperback book revolution.
10. School systems should make provisions for the kind of in-service education that will aid teachers to learn how to make the best use of paperback books.
11. Teachers, supervisors, and administrators should be alert to the many opportunities for correlation, integration and broad-field instruction afforded by the large-scale use of paperback books.

In recent years many meritorious innovations have appeared on the educational scene, but probably none so vital, dramatic, and far-reaching as the paperback book. Although the schools have only begun to utilize this tool, there will, in all probability, be much greater use of it in the future. Gradually, we predict, multiple paperback book editions will supplant the basal readers and single textbooks. It now remains for the classroom teacher and school administrator to take full advantage of this new form of magic.

The American Council of Learned Societies, in its 1964 *Report of the Commission on the Humanities,* stated: "The paperback revolution must be encouraged in the schools for it offers a partial solution to the problem of providing good printed materials."

An editorial in a New Jersey newspaper, the *Bergen Evening*

Record, in September 1965, stated the following after reading our study: "The case for the paperbacks is made. It is subscribed to not only by the New Jersey State Department of Education and the American Council of Learned Societies but by the people who count most—the school children. There could be no better endorsement."

It could be that all of us will live to retirement age or to be eighty-nine, as did the Japanese artist Hokusai and that, speaking our farewells to earthly scenes, we may paraphrase him, "If God had let us live five years longer, we might have helped in the improvement of the teaching of reading and in making school an interesting and dynamic experience."

PANEL DISCUSSION

When The Paperback Goes to School

WILLIAM D. BOUTWELL
Editorial Vice President,
Scholastic Magazines and Book Services, Inc.
and Moderator of the Panel

We used to talk of "the paperback revolution." That revolution in publishing and reading habits has won such wide acceptance that we now use a new term. You will find it in the title of this conference—"The Role of Paperback Books in Education." We no longer ask *when* paperbacks will be used in the schools; we ask *how*.

If we ask ourselves what sector of our population buys and reads the most paperbacks, the answer is: school children. At least one in every six paperbacks purchased in the United States today is bought by or for a child in elementary or secondary school. Children buy in school stores and through book clubs. They borrow paperbacks from libraries and read them on assignment. In some of our large high schools, it is not uncommon to find between 5,000 and 25,000 paperbacks going into student hands in a single year.

Our pollsters occasionally tell us that we are a nation of nonreaders, that only one in two reads a book in a year's time. They ask the wrong people. If they polled children and college students, and if they made clear that paperbacks, too, are books, they would come up with different statistics.

A few years ago, Scholastic Magazines and Book Services asked teenagers to send in photographs of how they read. We received hundreds of snaps. The best way to read, we learned, is lying on a bed with your feet up the wall. Or you can read on your stomach with the book on the floor. With a paperback you can read in a tree, or while washing dishes, or while milking a cow. Many read while taking a bath.

Some of the excitement children find in reading comes through in this not uncommon experience reported in the New

69

Jersey study on paperbacks. A fourth-grade child wrote why she liked paperbacks: "At night I'm always on a good chapter when I have to go to bed. So a minute after my light is out I get my flashlight and the book and read in bed." Mr. William Hinchliff of the Milwaukee Public Library could tell the pollsters what he found in neighboring high schools. Most students had personal paperback libraries ranging from fifty books up into the hundreds.

Not long ago one of my associates was dining with a *Reader's Digest* sales executive. The talk turned to the paperback book clubs, and the *Reader's Digest* man said, "I wonder if my youngsters know about this?" He called upstairs to his two teenagers: "Hey, up there, do you belong to a paperback book club?" Down came a reply in the condescending tone that children reserve for parents: "Of course we do. If you will just look in our rooms you will see we have heaps of paperbacks we bought at school."

Last year, the International Paper Company ran a splendid series of institutional advertisements to promote reading under the slogan, "Send me a man who reads." That is exactly what the teachers of this country are doing. By encouraging young people to read widely, by sponsoring book clubs and paperback book stores, and encouraging them to build personal libraries, the teachers have performed a kind of miracle.

In less than twenty years, the teachers—aided by librarians—have brought up a new generation that loves to read books. Currently the children of the United States read more books than any generation in our history. Their membership in book clubs far outnumbers enrollments in adult book clubs. Our children read more books than the children of any country at any time. So, to the International Paper Company, to every other industry, union, and institution, and to parents, the educators can say: "We are sending you young men and women who read. Furthermore, we believe we are sending you a generation that finds such pleasure and satisfaction in reading that they will go on reading throughout their lives."

We publishers of paperbacks—and that means practically all publishers—salute the educators for their achievement. We began to work with educators ten years ago, when a committee of the Metropolitan School Study Council invited some of us to a meeting here at Teachers College to hear their complaints about paperbacks. From this meeting grew the paperback committees of the American Book Publishers Council and the American Textbook Publishers Association. That early meeting also planted the seed of this conference, which was developed jointly by educators and publishers.

Proud as we are of the record, we should not let pride freeze into smug self-satisfaction and comfortable complacency. We have, in the paperback, something more than millions of words at discount prices.

"Media is the Message," declares Professor Marshall McLuhan. The paperback is not merely another book. It is a new medium, a new type of "message" for educators. It offers a book that can be owned rather than loaned. It offers printed materials that can be marked up and saved for future reference and use. It can separate the bulky and burdensome textbook into less formidable, lightweight parts. It gives both teacher and student opportunity to range widely and to individualize learning.

The road to knowledge is long and rocky. The textbook demands that students march the road in lockstep. The paperback, by contrast, invites exploration and assures more freedom of inquiry for the individual student. The paperback is not merely the same words in a less durable package. The paperback is a new medium, opening new doors for educators and students.

Students often say, "When it is in paperback, it seems shorter and easier to read."

If we ask whether educators have taken advantage of paperbacks as a new medium, the answer must be "no." This is the reason for this conference—to turn that "no" into a "yes."

What are the undeveloped frontiers on which we publishers wish to work with educators? I will list some of them:

1. Can administrators make it easier for teachers to use paperbacks? Can you review your acquisition policies and purchasing practices which were designed for hardcover books—mostly text-

books? Can you persuade your boards of education that it is not a crime to buy books that won't last five years? Can you persuade them that it is a good thing for students to own and cherish their school books?

2. Can administrators—where it is necessary—waive the restrictions on teachers collecting or assembling money for student purchase of books? These restrictions often stand in the way of children who want to buy books either through school stores or book clubs. The books these children want are usually not to be found in regular stores. Only the administrator and his school board can cut the red tape that sometimes keeps children and books apart.

3. Can librarians find it in their hearts to admit paperbacks to their libraries? Some of them do. In New Jersey, 64 per cent of the school libraries have paperbacks. Many librarians, however, still cling to the notion that a book is not a book unless it can be processed and checked in and out, has a hard cover, and lasts five years. Librarians could do much for children's reading and for teachers if they would open their doors to paperbacks—even sell them as do some librarians.

4. Can we—all of us—induce educators to read? The New Jersey study of paperbacks says: "It was often evident that many teachers knew very little about what books were appropriate for specific grade levels. It was found, too, that many were uninformed about recent professional publications and research data. An even more depressing revelation was the discovery that many teachers were themselves nonreaders and seldom read beyond the books used by their students." Other studies confirm this sad conclusion. Must we accept it as final? I think not. Twenty years ago, millions of children were nonreaders; today they are eager readers. Freedom of choice, easy availability, and low cost turned nonreaders into readers. Can we do for teachers what we have done for children? I believe so. The publishers would gladly join with education leaders to foster reading among educators.

5. Can paperbacks work in harness with textbooks? You will hear more on this from Mr. Rahtz.

6. Can we find ways and books to lure the children of the culturally deprived to reading? Some solution to this problem has been sought by Vice President Hubert Humphrey. He has sought the advice of publishers. Here is an aching and knotty problem calling for thought and action by the best minds in education, publishing, and government. Let's get going on this.

7. Can the benefits of inexpensive paperbacks for youth enjoyed in the United States be extended to other nations—especially the undeveloped nations? Here is a goal now far distant—even in Western Europe.

You will hear other problems presented by my fellow publishers. You have heard issues presented in section meetings. For my fellow publishers, I say this: We have given you a cornucopia of reading in paperback—35,500 titles in the 1965 *Paperbound Books in Print*. We are adding hundreds of new books every year. If we haven't satisfied your needs—and we know from experience that educators are never satisfied—let us know what you want. We stand ready to work with you individually or institutionally through our paperback committees. On one conviction I am sure we are in full agreement—reading not only maketh the full man but also the great society—by the way, that's a lower-case "g" and a lower-case "s."

Trade Paperbacks in the Schools

CHARLES G. BOLTÉ
Executive Vice President, The Viking Press

One of the most noticeable trends in the paperback field is that the differences between the mass-market publishers and the trade publishers are rapidly decreasing, in terms of both subject matter (we often find ourselves competing for the same books) and in prices (more and more mass-market books are costing over a dollar, as you are doubtless aware).

The situation we face is one of a generalized explosion. The population explosion after the war has now hit the colleges. There are, simply, more and more students to teach. We have a society becoming rapidly affluent, which means a higher proportion of the population can go to school and college. It also means they have more money to spend on books, as do local boards of education. We have a revolution in the entire governmental structure in which education and books are dealt with. The federal aid bills passed last year, as you all know, and this past session, are going to contribute enormously to the school budgets, and specifically to book budgets. That program, I think, will be continued and intensified in the future. After all, we have a President who was a teacher himself once and who, I think, would like to be known in the history books as a great teacher of the American people. His instincts are the same as yours. And he has selected as his Secretary of Health, Education, and Welfare a man who is perhaps the best-qualified professional in the country to carry out those instincts. Between LBJ and John Gardner there is going to be a lot of Federal support for education in the atmospherics as well as in the budget.

At the same time, publishers have been producing in paperback more and more titles that are suitable for school use, while educators have become more and more aware of the variety of titles, and of their possible use in the schools. All of these items

74

add up to a prospect which accounts for Wall Street's highly intensified interest in book publishing stocks in the last few years. The prospects are very good for more and bigger paperbacks. (Little paperbacks are getting bigger all the time.) There is a very considerable future in all of this development, and I see no reversal of the trends.

Of course, in the middle of a rapid growth period there are always growing pains. The two chief areas of pain, for both publishers and educators, are information and distribution. It is very hard to find out even what titles are available. I have yet to meet the man or woman who has read the 1965 edition of *Paperbound Books in Print* from cover to cover. It contains about eight hundred pages—over 35,500 titles, and they make no claim to having listed them all. There are more ways we can tell you what titles are available. There are more things that you, in your schools and in your school systems, ought to be doing to find out. No publisher can, on his own, get to all of you with information about the new titles, so you have to do some work by looking up the various media which list the new titles. It is very discouraging for publishers to go to school or library meetings and exhibits, see on display titles that have been available in paper for two, three, or four years, and then hear maybe half a dozen instructors say, in the course of the conference, "Oh, is *that* out in paper? I never saw it before." This happens all the time. I am not sure what we can do as publishers to get more information to you, but it is one of the chief areas of concern, and we are thinking about it all the time. More catalogs, I suppose, more direct mail, certainly more exhibits, and I hope more meetings like this around the country.

The other chief problem is distribution, which has been the perennial bugbear for American publishing all through the years. No matter in what form the books are published, there just are not enough book stores, not enough wholesalers. There are certainly not enough wholesalers who carry full lines of paperback books in particular. Frequently, the big wholesalers who are oriented traditionally toward schools and libraries are more cautious and conservative about paperback books than many educators are. And it is a real nuisance and a real burden for them to carry a full representation of paperback books when you consider how many titles there are and the enormous difference in the rate of sale of a title, depending on its current state of popularity, especially in the schools and colleges.

The worst aspect of distribution, of course, is receiving an order for a book that cannot be filled because the book is out of stock. Therefore, one specific suggestion I would like to make to teachers is this: When you know you are going to adopt a title, drop a postcard or a letter to the publisher and let him know, particularly if it is going to be a major purchase.

We knew the post-war baby boom was going to hit the colleges this fall, and we reprinted what we thought were adequate quantities of our major college best-sellers. But, by the end of August, we were out of stock on four of them, because the orders were so much bigger than we had expected. Many of the colleges did not warn us that (as far as I can tell) practically every freshman English course in the country would be reading *A Portrait of the Artist as a Young Man* this year. This demand is very gratifying, but we are distressed not to be able to fill the orders when they come in.

The distribution problem is, of course, intensified by the title proliferation problem, about which all of us are very much concerned. When is the bottom going to fall out of this thing? How much longer can we go on? No publisher will continue a title that is not reordered; yet you educators would like to see even more titles available—if you could find out what they were and if you could get them when you ordered them. It is likely that there will be some dropping out of titles in the future. The economics of the operation are such that we simply cannot afford to keep a title in print unless it sells a certain minimum number of copies a year—this number varying enormously from publisher to publisher.

However, despite what I just said about title proliferation, I think there will be more consciousness of your audience and your needs in books. You will get more reprints of young people's titles and juveniles and, I think, books designed for individualized learning and probably fewer general reprints, that is, in the higher priced area. The general market of readers that we all expected when the higher priced paperbacks came in has not developed as we had hoped, and most of us are now publishing largely for the educational market. Viking, as it happens, has been publishing primarily for the college market, but we are looking more and more to high school and even elementary.

I would like to close with one word about the freedom to read, censorship. I can see two trends there, one in the courts—a much more permissive attitude. It is very difficult to imagine a court nowadays defining anything as obscene or against the law, although there are still some courts that draw lines. But the general trend has been toward much more lenient treatment of anything the author wants to write about, as long as the judge thinks it has some redeeming social value, which covers a wide range of possible sins. At the same time, perhaps even as a result of this increasing permissiveness in the courts, we may see a trend toward more and more restrictive attitudes in the community, more and more local, voluntary, censorship groups, more and more police actions. I would urge all of you to consider this very much your business, as we consider it ours. The trouble with these things is that you also have to spend a great deal of time defending terrible books. I believe in the freedom not to read.

Trends in Paperback Books

OSCAR DYSTEL
President, Bantam Books

I represent the mass-distributed paperback book publishers on this panel. A mass-distributed paperback book is one which can usually be purchased for under a dollar, at a corner drugstore, at a supermarket, at an airport, or at other high traffic outlets. Without going into the long, detailed history, I think it suffices to say that the mass distributed paperback book has come a long, long way since it was first introduced to the American public through magazine channels of distribution, largely as a medium of pure escape and entertainment.

Speaking on an overall basis, I would say there have been three major areas in improvement. First, diversification in editorial effort; second, improvement in taste; third, improvement in production and distribution efficiency and technology. I might add the improvement in packaging. The shifting of editorial emphasis to fit the changing and growing needs of the market has been so vast in the last ten years that even those of us directly concerned with this industry tend to lose sight of what really has happened. Let me put it as clearly and simply as I can.

More than ten years ago, in the dim dark past of our industry's history, paperback books were mostly devoted to the more lurid variety of escapist reading, and most respectable people avoided mass-distributed paperbacks like the plague. But then the changes began to take place. First a whisper, then like a shout, and now a roar. We have discovered—perhaps by accident, and perhaps by design—that young people take to paperbacks like a bee takes to honey. Many of us, of course, wondered why, and we soon found out that the young people took to paperbacks because the books were friendly. These books were easy to carry; they were easy to handle; they were not stuffy, the youngsters said, and not imposing and intimidating like the traditional textbooks of the classroom. These discoveries were verified factually again and again in many surveys taken by various companies in the industry and by reports from teachers we met at conventions. Even more important, we discovered that young people wanted subject matter of a special nature, not necessarily the classics— but serious, qualitative, contemporary fiction, more reflective of the life and thoughts of this fast-moving century. They also were looking for books which would help them develop a greater understanding of the new frontiers of knowledge which had forcefully been opened for them through the power and scope of television and the ever-expanding curriculum of the secondary school.

These discoveries paved the way for completely revolutionized thinking on the part of publishers. New departments were organized with professional educators and staffs, and with an emphasis on marketing and publishing educational literature of a purely functional nature. The more titles we produced, the more we sold. There wasn't much organization to all of this in the beginning. It was more like a frontier land rush. We mass-distributing publishers all tried to get to the market first with the most and as a result our sales increase has been spectacular. Just let me give you a few figures.

According to industry surveys, the sales of mass-distributed paperback books to the educational market have increased since 1961 from about 22,000,000 units annually, to about 42,000,-000 in 1964. This is an increase of 20,000,000 units—or almost twice as many. We estimate that, in 1964, the industry sold about 325,000,000 units altogether and the sales of books primarily for educational buyers is estimated to be about 13 per cent of this total. However, with population increasing, with literacy improving, and with vast government support for educational programs in all areas, we publishers in the mass-distributed end of the books publishing industry expect the educational aspect of our business to soon surpass 30 per cent of our overall volume.

Now I would like to spend a few moments explaining just how the expansion in editorial content of paperback books has caused a remarkable chain reaction from groups of readers to groups of readers—and from one kind of simple distribution to a far more sophisticated kind of distribution. To us this chain reaction really has been amazing and fascinating to watch.

The acceptance of the paperback as a "real" book of good taste and as a medium of serious information has caused a remarkable growth in what we call the paperback store. Almost every major community in the United States today has an all-paperback retail outlet where one can find books on every conceivable subject. The growth of these outlets and the improved display of a wider array of titles have created more purchasing of paperback books and so this present period of expansion in the paperback industry is perhaps greater than at any time in history. Today you see people reading paperbacks everywhere— all kinds of people, at all socioeconomic levels, and reading all kinds of books.

I am sure you will agree that few groups are as conscious of fads and public habits as our children, whether they are young tots or young adults. The increase in reading among adults and in their own family circles has, in my opinion, had a profound effect on these youngsters. When the youngster sees his parents reading books and sees books all around him, he, too, tends to become a reader.

Educators for years have tried to establish the lifetime habit of good reading in children and young adults, yet this is very difficult to do if the home and community environment are devoid of books. Today, this condition does not prevail, since, with the mass-distributed paperback, each community has an opportunity never before available—and believe me, the parents and youngsters are taking advantage of it.

As you all probably know, there have been several local surveys—especially in New York City and the state of New Jersey—on the use of paperbacks in the schools. These surveys have reported favorable results when paperbacks were brought into the classroom. As I said earlier, I am not necessarily talking about *Huckleberry Finn* and *Great Expectations*. I refer to such books as *To Kill a Mockingbird, A Separate Peace, The Ugly American, Animal Farm, Brave New World* and *Of Human Bondage*. The intense desire of young people to "find themselves" in this modern world is inescapable. As a result, modern fiction has become very important to them. To-day, we find students choosing and successfully reading books that the curriculum would not have introduced to them a few years ago.

We also find, to our great and pleasant surprise, that the curriculum is catching up with the capabilities and interests of these young people and is adjusting to their reading tastes. There is more and more freedom in curriculum selection on a local level, and more and more teachers are developing greater aware-ness of the availability, in low-cost form, of fine literature. Thus, we find that the use of the mass-distributed paperback of quality is now increasing at an unprecedented rate. Just as an indication, paperback outlets within schools, which have become a tremendous factor in sales to school children of mass-distrib-uted paperbacks, now total approximately 7,500, and this figure is growing constantly. What better place can you think of to give the youngster the fingertip accessibility to mass-dis-tributed, low-priced paperbacks of quality?

I wonder whether you have all fully grasped the wide range of titles available, the tasteful packaging, the tremendous interest of paperback publishers in the educational market, and our de-sire as publishers to help. It was my purpose in the foregoing remarks to make you aware in a general way of what has hap-pened already. Just remember this figure—today there are over 35,500 different paperback titles in print on subjects for every conceivable taste.

As far as the future is concerned, all I can say is that we are just beginning in the educational field. We are constantly taking advantage of the greater speed in paperback publishing, and we are developing greater sophistication in the editorial aspects of our business, in order to keep abreast of the swiftly changing conditions of the classroom curriculum. Today many publishers have educational advisers associated with them, professionals who know what the curriculum requirements are. We are con-stantly going out among educators and attending educational conferences, to find out your changing needs and desires in this fast-moving world.

Of course, our goal is not only to develop sales in the educational market, but also to develop in these youngsters the lifetime habit of reading. Whole new areas of modern literature are becoming available to students, and new types of text materials are developing. Each publisher has his own program. Some publishers are examining the elementary school field; some publishers are concentrating on high schools and colleges; some publishers are trying to cover all markets. Each publisher is trying to get there first with the most, but I might add, with greater sophistication, greater know-how, and a greater sense of responsibility to the world of education. So the future of mass-distributed, low-priced paperbacks lies in the expansive areas from the lightest of leisure fiction to the most scholarly treatise —from teenage mysteries to the most definitive of textbook materials—from elementary school workbooks to programmed instruction—from bound magazine articles to the finest of prime source materials—from ancient scrolls to yesterday's television programs. Anything and everything you need to teach with the purpose of stimulating, building the habits of reading, thinking, questioning, and communicating will soon be available in mass-distributed paperbacks.

In conclusion, just let me say this. You people represent one of the most important keys to the success of this program. With your cooperation in communities everywhere, we will achieve the distribution of the better teaching materials in paperback form to the greatest number of students. But you must come forth and tell us what you want, what you need, and why you need it, and then you must endorse it by approving the use of paperback books in your schools. I think I can speak for every publisher here when I say our doors are open to you. Bring us your ideas and problems right from the classroom and we will produce the inexpensive materials you need for the classroom. If we work together, we can develop many, many of the proper reading tools to make possible the cultural revolution which we seek for the people of this country and which our young people today are demanding.

Paperback Textbooks in Our Schools

ROBERT RAHTZ
Vice President and Editor-in-Chief,
School Department, The Macmillan Company

A recent issue of *Publishers Weekly* contained a report of a conference at which some one hundred publishers were briefed by Dr. Marjorie C. Johnston, of the United States Office of Education, on federal funds for book purchases under the new Elementary and Secondary Education Act. Dr. Johnston is reported as saying that practically all types of materials will be eligible for purchase by schools under the Act, including the cost of *prebinding* paperbacks for school use. The word used here, note, is *prebinding,* not rebinding.

In other words, the new school law would make it possible for schools to buy paperback books, but would encourage them to use them as hardcover books. Or, to put it another way, a school would be able to use a book with the soul of a paperback and the body of a hardcover book.

This development seems to symbolize the ambiguous attitude that schools have long had towards paperbacks as textbooks. Schools seem interested in *principle* in paperbacks as tools of instruction, but they seem reluctant to *use* any but sturdily bound hardcover books.

And because of this attitude, largely, the number of paperback textbooks that are published for use in the elementary and high schools is still relatively small. It is not unusual for publishers to issue a high school textbook in two versions—hardcover and paperback. And, not infrequently, the hardcover version will far outsell the paperback.

This preference of school systems for hardcover books is, I suppose, understandable. Schools want to feel that when they invest in a book it will give them their money's worth with four or five years of wear—not only by surviving hard classroom use, but also by living through such subsidiary student uses as being second base in the school playground or the weapon of choice in whacking one's neighbor on the head.

However, today's paperback can be very sturdy physically; it can stand up under considerable hard wear. Improved adhesives are used in binding, and these, together with plastic-coated cover papers, result in books of very respectable durability.

Yet, the question of durability cannot always be analyzed simply by comparing the strength of a hardcover textbook with that of a paperback. Consider, for example, two high school literature series—one in the conventional hardcover format, with one large book per grade, the other a paperback series consisting of four volumes per grade. The hardcover book is designed to last four or five years. The paperback will, on the face of it, not last that long. But is this really true? Remember that one hardback text has to serve the student for an entire school year. In the paperback series, with four books devoted to a year's work, each book will be used during only one-fourth of the year. A teacher who uses the paperback series can issue the paperback books to a student one at a time, and recall them for storage when that book has been read. In the course of four years, then, each of the paperbacks will receive a total of only four quarter-years' use, compared with the full four or five years' use of the hardcover anthology. Schools concerned with the economics of textbook purchasing would do well to investigate this aspect of the use of paperback textbooks.

But dollars and cents do not necessarily tell the whole story. Returning again to the comparison of the two literature programs, we might note that the four paperback books contain roughly 40 per cent more text material than the single-volumed, hardcover anthology. Thus, the teacher has at her disposal a fuller program in literature. She can pick and choose from among the materials in the paperbacks according to the tastes and interests of her students and herself. The selections that are not covered in class can be assigned as additional work. Certainly this fuller, more flexible program, available at no higher cost than the hardcover textbook, is much in keeping with today's trend towards richer, more extensive text materials.

While the publication of basic textbooks for elementary and high schools has moved slowly, the publication of another kind of material by textbook companies has developed much more rapidly and extensively. I am referring to what are generally called supplementary textbooks. Supplementary textbooks may be used in several ways. One way is in support of a basic hardcover textbook—to amplify certain portions, to provide a different point of view. A second way is to use these supplementary textbooks in place of the basic, hardcover book. In the past few years large numbers of such supplementary paperback books have been published by textbook firms, particularly in the fields of American history, language arts, mathematics, and science. I think it worth noting that many of the curriculum study groups, such as SMSG, PSSC, and BSCS, have provided for the publication of paperbacks as part of their work.

I anticipate a steady growth in the use of supplementary paperbacks—both those specially prepared by textbook companies and regular trade paperbacks that have relevance to school courses. This seems to me to be a healthy development for schools as well as for publishers. First it signifies a willingness of teachers to abandon complete reliance on one hardcover textbook for all their students. I believe that American textbooks, by and large, do a good job of teaching and conveying information, but at the same time I think it is important for students to go beyond the textbook to other sources for additional material and differing points of view. In this way, students will be led to realize that one book cannot and should not be regarded as gospel. Second, the growth in the use of supplementary paperbacks is a sign of increasing professional competence on the part of our teachers. After all, a teacher who successfully conducts her course using a variety of materials requires more pedagogical skill to accommodate the variety of information and points of view than the teacher who slavishly and unimaginatively follows a single textbook.

The future of supplementary paperbacks is a bright one. The future for basic paperback textbooks may be bright as well, but only if people like yourselves are successful in conveying your enthusiasm to the school administrators who are responsible for setting policy on book purchases. When the effective demand for such texts becomes widespread, publishers will, I am sure, respond. Perhaps they will take their cue from American automobile manufacturers who were faced with stiff competition a few years ago from foreign-made compact cars. With the American automobile-buying public insisting on compact cars, American manufacturers responded by producing, if not better, certainly bigger, compacts.

GROUP   DISCUSSIONS

Synthesis of Group Discussions

FRANK G. JENNINGS
Education Consultant,
The New World Foundation

The fifty-two workshop discussion groups which met during the paperback book conference provided opportunities for teachers, administrators, editors, publishers, authors, and researchers to talk together and to explore the programs and practices relating to the use of the paperback book in education. Many of these discussion groups had opportunities to respond to prepared statements or short papers dealing with the specific issue or area of the individual group. This section is an attempt to synthesize both the papers and the discussions. Although we are forced, because of the large number of active participants, to present this material anonymously, it should be read with the understanding that this is quite literally the voice of the people who are involved in education.

I hope what follows will accurately convey the variety of interests of the participants, the range of their programs, and the depth of their commitment to the exploitation of the paperback in all of its relevant forms in the tasks of teaching and learning. It would be manifestly impossible, within the scope of a single section, to provide a detailed account of the work of each of the groups, for they were essentially teaching and learning sessions themselves. I have made the editorial decision to synthesize and to summarize this work and to provide a usable running account of the interplay of ideas. The purpose of this section is to enable the general reader, out of his or her own interests and experience, to grasp the broader aspects of the issues and the discussions. Finally, it is to be hoped that the remaining sections, most especially the one dealing with case studies, can be read with the perspective thus gained.

The General Advantages of the Paperback in Education

Paperback books in general can provide a range of learning experiences greater than any single textbook or even a textbook series. This is especially true in literature, the social studies, and the sciences. Paperback books are especially valuable in providing documentary material of a far greater scope than one could expect in a single textbook. A carefully annotated title list in a given area can provide background and structure for a course of study which the individual teacher can tailor to the specific needs of the student. Such lists can provide greater perspective and more opportunity to make comparisons among different and divergent viewpoints and to establish relationships among ideas and events. They can also provide in-depth treatment, as well as up-to-date discussion, on almost any topic that comes under examination in the classroom.

If the teacher has access to a sufficiently wide range of titles it will be possible to account for and to deal with the wide range of abilities and interests to be found in the classroom. There are implications here, of course, for individualized instruction, as well as for individualized reading programs. There is implied further the opportunity to put into operation Jerome S. Bruner's thesis that any child can be taught any subject at any stage of his development in some educationally legitimate fashion.

Perhaps one of the most significant strengths of the paperback in the classroom is that it can be *possessed* by the student. It can be written in; sentences and paragraphs can be underlined; the student can engage the author in critical discussion. In short, the paperback book can be read as closely and as positively as Mortimer J. Adler has suggested books should be read, in his own book (available, of course, in paperback) entitled *How to Read a Book*.

Finally, although some teachers and librarians are discomfited by the art work on some of the covers, it is generally agreed that the paperback is attractive precisely because of its variety, its portability, and its lack of fierce formality. In short, there's nothing stuffy or dour about the little book.

Teaching Style and the Use of Paperbacks

The use of paperbacks gives an opportunity for more freedom and responsibility in teaching style. Some see this as an advantage, and others as a hazard. The teacher who has an opportunity to use paperbacks is free. But this is a freedom with a cost attached. The hardcover textbook may limit the teacher; it can also protect him. In fact, the often unstated editorial policy upon which a textbook is based is that the teacher either does not want or is unable to range freely through the subject matter dealt with in the book. With a paperback list, the teacher must at all times attempt to maintain some significant mastery of the subject matter. This inevitably demands of the teacher professional habits of work that can be as onerous as they are challenging. Paperbacks do not *work* by themselves, the way carefully prepared textbooks do. There are no helpful little sections entitled "Something to Think About," "Things to Do," or "Related Ideas." There are no formal little end-of-chapter tests, no intrusive (or supporting) footnotes, except as the author, who usually has written with no thought for the classroom teacher's problems, has felt it necessary to expand upon or explain a point.

While it is true that there are some teachers who see the rich resources of the paperback lists as a way of driving the textbook out of the classroom, there are many others, clearly in the majority, who do not see this as either a desirable or inevitable consequence. For them the textbook has its place, perhaps as the backbone of the course, or as a dependable curriculum guide. The paperback does provide collateral reading, enrichment, the rounding out of the parsimonious text. There are other educators, though few in number, who urge the inclusion of textbook features in the paperback, and they have not been unsuccessful, for there are today an increasing number of paperbacks which include vocabularies, glossaries, and teaching aids.

Some administrators, both at the paperback book conference and elsewhere, have expressed doubts about teachers' ability to to effectively organize their own courses. Some, in fact, see the possibility of curriculum chaos in which each teacher goes his or her own way with no regard either for guidelines or for the programs of his colleagues in earlier or later grades. There are warnings, too, from administrators and supervisors that the beginning teacher especially needs more support, more guidance, and even more control than would be possible in programs employing paperback books exclusively. Some teachers frankly support these viewpoints, saying, in effect, that they have some doubts about their own ability to make appropriate use of materials of such flexibility. They warn that merely to change materials or to provide greater freedom in their use is no guarantee that the free teacher will be liberated to do her job.

Some teachers, on the other hand, question their ability to provide adequate direction and control of the classroom program and are concerned, too, with the difficulty of evaluating the results of their efforts. The traditional textbook does provide some guarantees in these areas, whether real or imagined. It does ensure against inappropriate duplication of program and material, and, if it is part of a series, it also provides for articulation and coordination within a secure curriculum framework. Finally, some of the newer textbook series have been adapted to meet the needs of the slow learner and the disadvantaged child.

Countering the so-called advantages of hardcover textbooks and series, however, is the urgent insistence of those who espouse the freedom offered by the paperback lists. They insist that individualized reading programs can provide the guidelines and the controls necessary, can establish adequate means of evaluation, and can bring to the teaching-learning enterprise the excitement which it must have and which is so often lacking in the classroom.

There are, however, other demurrers raised concerning the dangers of "unselected" material. And this refers both to questions of censorship and appropriateness of selection. For who is to decide what is "good" or "bad" literature? Who is to decide what is desirably controversial and what is undesirably distorted? Who is to monitor the language and the situations to be found in novels that have not been screened either by an editor or by a textbook selection committee?

Obviously, these questions raise certain larger, philosophical issues—issues before which many teachers and administrators feel very uncomfortable. These issues, if they are not resolved, can disturb the day-to-day work of the classroom, for they come down to the point of questioning whether or not the classroom teacher can effectively participate in formulating curriculum policy.

Many teachers in the conference returned often to the issue of freedom, both for themselves and for the student. For freedom involves both the right and the responsibility of choice, and choice demands that one live with the consequences of one's decisions. This, in turn, forces one to consider the very structure of the curriculum itself. For example, one participant suggested that the wealth of material presented in paperback books demands the elimination of the older, departmental labels, such as "history" and "social studies," in favor of larger classifications, such as the "humanities." Within this framework, students and teachers could make use of the many specialized paperbacks in such areas as philosophy, history, and cultural anthropology. There would then be demanded of the teacher a level of understanding and a degree of involvement both in subject matter and in the conduct of the class that few teachers have yet achieved or accepted.

In the final analysis what can be said of the teacher must be also said of the student, for the richness of the paperback lists provides at every level opportunities for free inquiry far greater than have hitherto been available to the student, whatever his age or ability.

Paperbacks and the Individual Needs of Students

Paperback books are particularly welcomed by educators who see in them great resources in providing appropriate motivation to students, while at the same time respecting their individuality and their social and psychological needs.

There is a tendency to look upon paperbacks as a sovereign

remedy for specific ills or problems. The slow learner, the disadvantaged child, the gifted child, and the underachiever all are looked upon as representing unique opportunities through which to test the efficacy of new materials and new approaches. Thus, not only the paperback book, but educational television, language laboratories, programmed instruction, and the whole range of so-called new educational technology are often considered with the needs of these specific children in view.

There were many occasions on which participants in the workshops did discuss paperbacks as remedial materials for specific educational problems. More often, however, the discussions were kept in the larger educational perspective. While it is recognized that the wise use of paperbacks by the teacher can enable students to discuss and question viewpoints and values expressed in the books and to deal with their own reactions openly and freely, it was equally recognized that this is possible with any book, or for that matter, with any other communication medium, be it film, radio, or television. The point to be stressed, however, is that the paperbacks are generally inexpensive, can be made more readily available, can be assembled in very flexible groupings, and can allow greater scope in the design of programs to meet special needs.

One may well ask the almost rhetorical question, "Are paperbacks effective with slow learners?" It is conceivable that a well-chosen selection may be an answer to the frustration which existing textbook anthologies generally present to these children. It is thought, with some justification, that the slow learner is usually concerned with the immediate and practical world he comes to grips with every day. It is generally considered that slow learners have to be dealt with individually and do not respond easily to mass instruction. The effective teacher could have, with easy access to paperback lists, a ready source of reading matter that would be efficacious in the teaching of such children. There are, however, drawbacks to be found in most of the presently available paperbacks—for example, narrow margins, closely printed pages, generally unattractive and sometimes difficult typography, and poverty of illustration. That such drawbacks could be remedied is unquestioned, but that the cost of the remedies might defeat the editorial aims of paperback production must also be considered.

When one turns to the special problems attendant upon the teaching of the culturally disadvantaged, many discussants emphasized the following: The disadvantaged are not necessarily slow learners; they are cut off from the world of books. Educators must involve them, by making books available in as many situations as possible, in all parts of the school; by having older children read to them; by giving them books they can take home. It is especially fruitful to offer these children a great variety of material. They need more, not less material, in order to comprehend. But it is especially important with these children to have clearly and simply stated goals, which is perhaps more difficult if you are working with a great variety of material.

These observations suggest an editorial problem and an editorial opportunity. Some teachers believe, with considerable reason, that both the disadvantaged child and the slow learner dislike "big" books because they look harder and longer. Anthologies that are illustrated with pictures that are irrelevant in the lives of such children are sources of frustration. The editorial problem, then, is to find, or cause to be written, stories and material that are relevant in the lives of these children and to present this writing in formats that will be both attractive and significant. On the other hand, there is always available considerable evidence that good writing and great stories, regardless of the format or the complexity of the language, can be made accessible to these children, and that merely to tailor-make a "product" for these children is to avoid the central issue of effective teaching and significant curriculum design. It comes down, finally, to the issue of whether or not it is possible to cull from the great list of titles the stories and textbooks in which these children can find characters with whom to identify, situations within which they can live imaginatively, and information about the real and fantastic worlds that can awaken the interest of children who are usually disbarred from the goods of society.

Effective Ways of Presenting Paperbacks to Students

It is too often forgotten in discussing the paperback that before and after one talks about its special qualities it remains what it essentially is—a book. What is special about the paperback is that it permits the freer use of a book than has been usual in the past. Classroom libraries are easier to assemble; central libraries can be more cheaply enlarged and maintained; and the special virtues of the book, whatever they are, can be exploited more fully.

Thus, the question asked in some of the groups, "Is there any special need to prepare students for the use of paperbacks, and how may this be done?," is recognized as an old question, addressed to an old and excellent instrument.

One "prepares" students for the use of books by creating an atmosphere of interest and acceptance; by relating what is available to the individual interests and needs of the student; and by connecting the students' other language and their aesthetic and social experiences to the literary experience that awaits them on the printed page.

To make the best use of these books, which happen to be paperbacks, we must put them where the students are; the books must be available and in sight, whether in the classroom or in the library. The fact that they are paperbacks, with certain unique economic virtues, suggests that they can be "used up." This is a theme which recurred in many discussion groups and throughout the conference as a whole.

Teachers can and should promote the possession of books, and this can be done with the paperback. For the disadvantaged child, especially, it is not enough merely to have the books made available to him. He needs the books in his home, as possessions of himself and of his family. This is necessary because, to the extent that the parents can find significance in the possession of books, the child's opportunity for academic success is enhanced. This has been demonstrated in many places throughout the country, perhaps most dramatically in the Phillips Brooks House (Harvard University) Book Exposure Program in Boston.

There are many strategies one may employ for getting books into these homes. One can devise paperback book clubs and paperback book fairs with special programs to ensure that the books get into the home and are used there. The New Jersey paperback book program, which is described elsewhere in this book, has many such suggestions. The use of carefully designed summer reading programs is also an effective means of connecting the family and the child to the book and to the school.

It should always be remembered, however, that one cannot talk about books in the abstract. Books are language experiences that take place among other language experiences—the film, radio, television, popular songs. It is important to recognize and exploit this fact. One must learn to choose a book not in place of another experience, such as television or a movie, and not merely in addition to such an experience, but as a unique experience in itself. Sometimes the teacher unconsciously cheats when he says, "You've seen the movie (or the television show); now read the book." This is like comparing eggs and oranges. The only thing they have in common is that they are both edible. The teacher is advised to be aware of as many of the language experiences to which the child is exposed as possible and to make every effort to connect these experiences without prejudicing any one of them. The current educational jargon term "multi-media" is a piece of arrant nonsense which attempts to label a vast array of experiences. The inappropriateness of the term is indicated in the fact that it is assembled from two word fragments, both of which mean plurality.

Although elsewhere in this volume there is an extensive discussion of specific programs, the following description of some pilot projects is given as an indication of the variety of ways in which the paperback can be put to use in education and as an illustration of some of the ideas presented in these discussions.

The Fraser Valley Regional Library in British Columbia put adult paperbacks into seventeen branch libraries. Young people flocked to the adult paperbacks, and as a consequence use of the children's library declined, so the children's libraries were then stocked with paperbacks. However, most thirteen- to fifteen-year-olds continued to prefer the adult collections. Many of these teenagers were first attracted into the library by the paperbacks. In general this library does not place any restrictions on the use of adult books by children; this atmosphere of freedom especially appeals to early teenagers.

In the "open" English curriculum of Monmouth Regional High School, New Shrewsbury, New Jersey, there is no required course of study or required reading list. The teachers choose from a list of paperback titles, on the basis of their assessment of students' abilities and interests. Some guidance is provided to teachers to ensure sequence and adequate coverage of skills and content.

The New York City Board of Education has developed its own paperback science textbooks for seventh through ninth graders, and these books are given to the students to keep. They are tailor-made to the curriculum, can be kept current, and can be used by the student as he wishes. New York City hopes to develop future programs like this, for both disadvantaged and gifted studens.

The Plandome Road Elementary School in Manhasset, Long Island, put paperbacks on sale in the library. It was found that poor or reluctant readers, especially, gravitated to the paperbacks and that many students through their experiences with paperbacks became interested in hardcover books.

"English in Every Classroom," which began in a training school in Michigan, is now being started in a number of metropolitan school systems in the East and Middle West. In this program the responsibility for teaching English is diffused throughout every classroom and every subject. The curriculum is "saturated" with newspapers, magazines, and paperbacks, and the paperback book is used as the primary text; this induces the child not only to learn to read, but to like to read.

Paperbacks in the Subject-Matter Fields

Much of the discussion about the appropriateness of the paperback book in the subject-matter fields stems from dissatisfaction with the quality and the scope of existing textbooks and other materials. In this context it often appears as if the paperback represents a chance to start anew. In others, however, a more moderate position is taken which sees the paperback as valuable collateral support to the textbooks or series that are in use.

ENGLISH

Most of the discussion in the groups appeared to stem from the desire of the English teacher to "get rid of the anthologies." This is an old complaint among English teachers. Anthologies are seen to present snippets and pieces of literature, rather than opportunities for full reading experiences. The standard anthologies are criticized for their mechanical structure, their heavy use of gratuitous footnotes, and their ever-present hints, suggestions, and "things to do," which some teachers look upon as curriculum straitjackets. The paperback book is seen as a way of breaking out, for both the teacher and the student. One teacher asks, for example, "Why do we challenge the word of a child and feel that we must question him about every book he reads? Reading should be a joyous activity."

One special advantage of the paperback for both teacher and student is that it makes available an almost full range of modern literature, in contrast to the anthology textbook, which depends more on the "tried and true classics" and is often governed by reprint-rights costs of newer materials. For example, a short story by Hawthorne can be reprinted at no cost, since it is out of copyright. Any story published initially within the last fifty-six years carries a reprint cost which increases the production cost of the book.

Another virtue of paperbacks in the English curriculum is that they can provide vigorous models for the teaching of composition. It was strongly suggested that by their use it should be possible to effect a remarriage of the teaching of literature and of composition within the curriculum. Again, this suggestion appears to come from a hope for another chance, though some teachers see it as simply the means whereby the classroom teacher can assert his or her legitimate curriculum autonomy.

SOCIAL STUDIES

The social studies curriculum has been in ferment for almost a decade. New materials and new approaches to the handling of older materials have been coming from research centers, curriculum teams, and the editorial offices of the big publishing houses. The classroom teachers' view, however, is still that the social studies classroom is dominated by the standard text. Whether the view is narrow or not, the teacher's response is to turn to the paperback literature in order to find material that is more specifically relevant to the needs of the students and the world in which they live.

As does the English teacher, the social studies teacher looks upon the paperback as a way of getting beyond the tired recitation of facts and of providing contexts within which documents, biographical material, and the literature of the historical periods can be woven together. Many teachers see opportunities, here, to involve the student in a personal encounter with history and, consequently, to develop in him a sensitivity to analysis and to questions of purpose and value. Thus, some teachers see the chance for the social studies to regain some of the ground in "citizenship education," which they feel has been lost in recent years.

HUMANITIES

Although it is rare for the humanities to be formally associated with a secondary-school curriculum, there is increasing interest in developing a legitimate place for them. Once again, by talking about the wealth of material in the paperback lists, teachers in the discussion groups were able to discuss, not whether something called "the humanities" should be taught, but rather the idea that humanistic concerns, since they are implicit in the total curriculum, can and must be dealt with explicitly.

The point was made that man "needs to find his own answers to life," and that the attempt to do so involves knowing how to ask questions that are appropriate. One needs to find connections between what one reads and what one experiences as one encounters art objects and art events, and what all of this has to do with life as it is lived. There was considerable excitement in these discussions, reflected in such statements as "You need to find out about other people's experiences to know what humanity is." Such a search cannot be made through any single textbook or any single course, however well conceived. A great variety of materials, activities, and experiences must be woven together and given some order. The teacher must have a point of view with respect to such engagements and be in a position both to express that viewpoint, whatever it is, and to use it as a way of introducing the students to dealing with the greater questions of life, loyalty, reality, beauty, and truth.

FOREIGN LANGUAGES

The role of the paperback in the learning of foreign languages does not differ from its role in other areas, except that there is not yet available a rich enough supply of textbooks and materials to be used in the school. The paperback has a long and honored history and tradition in Europe. It is tempting to consider the consequences of its greater exploitation in books reprinted by American publishers, either in their original language and format or in bilingual editions. This could be done at all levels of instruction. It would make possible a greater use of reading experience in language study than is usually the case. The learning of a language is not accomplished through contact with a single book, but, rather, through the accumulation of many experiences in reading, speech, and thought. It is in reviewing these experiences that previous learning is reinforced until a level of competence is reached that will allow the student free access to the literature of the language. As in every other area the teachers see that the paperback presents an important way of promoting this by making it possible for the students to own their own books.

The teachers in the discussion groups were very insistent that the publishers be urged to experiment, especially in the area of foreign language vocabulary levels and interest levels, which, it was pointed out, are very rarely specified by the publishers.

SCIENCE

The wealth of materials available in paperbacks in the sciences is far richer for curriculum purposes than in any other area, but this very richness presents problems of selection and use. The developments and changes in secondary science curricula, as well as the innovation in the use of science in the elementary school, make it very important that the teacher be given guidance in selection and use.

The point was made in the discussion groups that the science paperbacks make it possible for the teacher to teach science in a manner more consistent with the nature of the scientific enterprise than has hitherto often been the case. It is important to refer to what is called the "cumulative aspect of science," the necessity to draw upon and check with the work of others dealing with the same or similar problems, and to evaluate conflicting sources of information.

There were also clear indications that connections must be made for the student between the sciences and the humanities.

The richness of the paperback literature in science was cited many times for its sharp contrast with the quality of material available in traditional science education. For instance, the vocabulary restriction in elementary science books prevents the introduction of essential terms and concepts. The so-called general science area offers meager intellectual fare, and there is rarely any adequate exploitation of the science experiences that are available to children via television and through science games and toys.

The foregoing discussion, although not exhaustive, points to the particular appropriateness of paperback books to the kind of educational world the teachers see emerging. It is a world in which there will be greater autonomy and independence for both teacher and student, greater variety of experience, less regimentation, more respect for and emphasis on individuality—a world in which the teacher will have more opportunity to be both guide and mentor.

These are educational ideals which all too often have been reduced to platitudes and clichés but which, nontheless, have lost neither their validity nor their capacity to inspire. Teachers will always respond to new possibilities for instruction, as they have responded in the past to the film, to radio, and to television. Although the possibilities are rarely realized in their fullness, some of their generative power does become attached to the affairs of the classroom. So today teachers have gone beyond the excitement of "the paperback revolution" and see again the opportunity to teach children how to learn on their own. For the world ahead of us, with its increased leisure time and its accelerating changes in work opportunities, will be hospitable to the citizen who is as open to change as the society itself is prone to change. The capacity for continuing education has always been enhanced in direct proportion as books are available to the general reader. The classrooms of a nation are strong in direct proportion as the varieties of literature are directly accessible to teacher and student.

It is with thoughts of this kind, with educators meeting in the discussion groups talking about the paperback in the subject-matter areas, that a new kind of school program was seen as emerging. It will be a program, said the teachers, emphasizing individual progress, independent study, flexible programming— a program demanding wide and diversified reading at all levels and in all grades, rather than slavish dependence upon single textbooks, anthologies, or series. As the teachers made these observations and explored the consequences, they were conscious of saying again what had been said before, but there was a feeling that there were differences both in the quality of opportunity and in the probability that the opportunity will be seized.

Paperbacks and the School Library

The increasing emphasis in education on individualized instruction and the growth in extent of academic programs, with the resulting need for more and more materials of all kinds, means that libraries must drastically enlarge their collections. Paperbacks can help them do this.

This means that librarians must get away from the custodial tradition, in which books are regarded as unique and irreplaceable—as permanent records that must be passed on to succeeding generations. Many librarians find the idea of paperbacks objectionable, as they have misgivings about their content, believe they are easily lost to the library, and fear that lack of durability and the expense of conventional methods of processing and circulation might diminish any initial economic advantage. However, some librarians have suggested that less elaborate systems of handling would be more appropriate for paperbacks.

The decision to include paperbacks in the school library presents the necessity of considering the many ways in which this can be done. For instance, paperbacks can replace the hardcover book collection, in order to offer more books. Or they can be offered for special purposes for which hardcovers are not so appropriate, such as supplying current materials in rapidly changing fields or concerning current events of high interest over a short period of time.

It has been pointed out that the use of paperbacks—whether in the library or elsewhere—increases the use of books in general, including library books. However, since paperbacks are now being used to build both classroom and personal libraries, some teachers and librarians are now finding it important to consider more carefully the function of the central school library. One librarian felt that the increasing use of paperbacks would ultimately bring about a situation in which libraries will serve only for "work," that is, as a repository for reference materials, not as a place for reading as a pursuit in itself. At least one teacher saw an advantage of paperbacks in enabling a student to do individual research without having to cope with library restrictions.

Beyond this is the question of whether in the future it will be useful to have central school libraries. In general it was felt that paperbacks will change the role of the librarian from that of maintaining a central depository to one of serving as a consultant on books for the teacher and for the individual student who wants to own books. For example, the librarian can help teachers to keep up with titles and suggest books to meet individual needs. She can assemble classroom collections of paperbacks dealing with specialized areas of study. One teacher went so far as to predict that the central school library would be replaced by a paperback book store run by a trained professional as part of the instructional program of the school.

The Financing of Paperbacks

There seems to be no evidence that the paperbacks are relatively more expensive to use than hardcovers. Sometimes the argument is made that paperbacks are cheaper "because there is no problem of storing and making sure that they are returned to the school." But this implies acceptance of the notion that the paperback book is absolutely expendable. School management often dictates quite the reverse, as anyone who has experience with ephemeral materials can testify. (Many school journals now advertise kits for making permanent bindings for paperbacks!) It should be noted that the very term "paperback" itself covers a vast array of very different kinds of books, some of which are as well made as any clothbound volume, the only difference being in the cover.

There was general agreement in the discussion groups, however, that, whatever the complexity of the economics, the various educational advantages are so great that the use of the paperback ought not to be determined on economics alone. It was reported that one school system sees in the very lack of long-term durability a very simple advantage, in that it permits the easier elimination of unsuccessful titles.

Several times the issue of textbooks and paperbooks was discussed. The majority opinion seemed to be that a textbook bound in paper was still a textbook and was precisely "what we want to get away from." A more moderate and at the same time perhaps more sophisticated point of view welcomes the paperbound textbook for precisely the same reasons that the general book is found desirable; it can be made expendable; it can be marked up, worked in, and quickly discarded when it is out of date.

Another financial aspect, referred to earlier in this section, is the cost of improving upon the often unattractive typography, limited variety of format, and usual absence of attractive illustrations. It remains to be seen whether remedying these drawbacks will destroy some of the paperback's special economic efficacy.

Finally, where is the money for paperbacks coming from? Teachers, administrators, and librarians in the discussion groups reported on the difficulties of getting local tax monies allocated to the purchase of paperbacks. They report that this difficulty is due partly to the "bad image" the paperback has in the public eye and in some instances even to censorship pressures from special interest groups. However, the more fundamental issue seems to be the need for better information about the advisability of investment in paperbacks. The public has to be informed that the paperback can, in its own way, provide as adequate service as the hardcover book can.

Under Titles I, II, and III in the Elementary and Secondary Education Act of 1965 it should be possible to secure federal funds for paperbacks. There is need for school people and for the public to have more specific information on the use of these sources and their limitations, and publishers would be well-advised to provide this information.

Paperbacks and the Professional Growth of Teachers

Both university presses and commercial publishers have been producing more and more titles specifically directed to the professional educator. These titles include many that hitherto have been available only with great difficulty, through central libraries or at prices far higher than most teachers have been willing to pay. The richness of resource that the paperback in general represents is even more clearly displayed here, for in addition to the general cultural and intellectual treasure, an ever-increasing flow of technical material, monographs, and research reports now finds its way to the teacher in paperback form. It is possible today, as it has never been in the past, for almost any teacher, no matter how isolated from cultural and intellectual centers, to acquire and maintain a personal professional library of sufficient scope to meet his professional needs. What is more important, however, and what has been stressed time and again in these discussion groups, is that the paperback provides the teacher with the means of a genuine, continuing, professional education, not only in his specific field of interest, but in those other areas of inquiry and exploration of which the modern teacher must be aware.

The Right Paperback at the Right Time for the Right Student

This is an old cry with a slightly new accent. And it represents the perennial problem of the teacher and the student. How, indeed, can one evaluate and select wisely useful titles from the endless flood of paperbacks? Where can one turn for guidance? Whose list will you accept? Or, for that matter, whose list can you trust? Ideally, of course, every teacher should develop a specific list for a specific class, and every teacher should have the knowledge and the courage—I might almost say the intellectual wealth—to discard even the best list he or she has ever devised, simply because there are new books and new boys and girls. This is not to say that books appearing on earlier lists would have no place on later lists. It is simply to recognize that, as the teacher deals with a continuing flow of information about books, which may or may not be relevant to the task of teaching, that teacher is engaged in his own continuing education, and some of the results of that education are profitable to himself and his students.

In the discussion groups some of the consultants, in response to questions about lists, offered the information with appropriate hesitancy, warning in several instances that these lists had not been editorially "tested" as textbooks, on the contrary, always are. An important educational issue is immediately raised here. Textbook publishers, however they may be criticized for their shortcomings as well as for their overreaching, nonetheless have provided generations of American teachers and school children with orderly guidance, with carefully tested materials, and with all kinds of ancillary support for the programs their textbooks were designed to enhance. With the paperback book there is no such service, except in those instances where the paperback is a textbook wearing a different dress. The issue that is raised, then, is whether or not the classroom teacher is in a position to exercise those critical functions which the textbook publisher provides automatically.

If the teacher is willing and able to select the titles, to assemble them in an appropriate array, and to provide the editorial apparatus to make that collection pedagogically sound, can such a teacher assume this function and concurrently carry on the day-to-day business of teaching? The question is only partly rhetorical because it implies a level of teacher education that so far has been rarely achieved. It implies, furthermore, a degree of teacher autonomy that is rarely accorded the classroom teacher. Finally, it implies a level of freedom from pressures both within the school administration and from the community at large that is almost never guaranteed to today's teacher. In short, there is implied in these questions an implicit revolution in teacher education that has not yet been adequately described.

The classroom teacher is supported in the choice of books and other instructional materials by many different kinds of specialists and several ranks of administrators and supervisors. This support can free the teacher to carry on the business of the classroom. It can also smother the individual initiative and creativity of the teacher under a bureaucratic blanket of do's and don'ts. The resourceful, well-prepared, well-educated teacher always manages to preserve his essential professional integrity. The lazy teacher does not care. The inept and inexperienced teacher rarely knows what is happening to him. What the members of the discussion group repeatedly returned to was the opportunity and the burden that free access to paperbacks entails.

The services that have been and are available to the classroom teacher will continue, as they should. But, in addition, the teacher is being thrown more and more upon his own resources. These resources must be enlarged. This requires that his own education, both undergraduate and professional, must prepare him to assume the larger risks and responsibilities that our cultural and technological affluence make inescapable. There is an implication here that one of the things the public has a right to expect is that the teacher will be a well-read person, in the old-fashioned meaning of that phrase, and that he will also be continuously engaged in his own education. This means also that he will be "engaged" in his society in the sense that he is aware of and responsive to major currents in thought and major issues in social policy, as well as the minor trends, shifts, and fads of popular life. This is not to say that one can ascribe to the so-called paperback revolution responsibility for generating this new level of expectation on the part of the public towards the teaching profession. That "revolution" is, however, one very significant aspect in a fundamental shift in attention towards educational matters that has been developing in this country over the past decade.

The classroom teachers who attended the paperback conference were in very many instances representative of this enlarged and enhanced professional attitude. The questions they raised and the issues they explored relative to the use of the paperback demonstrated, in most instances, a willingness and an ability to accept the challenges.

CASE STUDIES

Case Studies

Vice President, Scholastic Magazines and Book Services, Inc.

As soon as the paperback appeared on our cultural horizon, teachers and librarians began to discover its advantages as a new resource for improving education. The many scholastic journals are filled with descriptions of teacher use of paperbacks for a wide variety of purposes—for bright students and slow students; for students in science, English, history, and other subjects; for the encouragement of personal libraries; and for supplementing textbooks. Educators have told about paperbacks in school stores, in book clubs, and in book fairs.

The following case studies have been chosen from a broad range of personal testimony. Examples were selected to demonstrate uses of paperbacks at every level of elementary and secondary schools. In addition to being examples of how paperbacks have been used by teachers in various subject areas for students with all sorts of special characteristics, the cases demonstrate the ingenious ways in which educators solve distribution problems.

All through these accounts run the threads of joy and satisfaction that teachers, librarians, and students experience in discovering that paperbacks open new vistas of delight in reading books.

Classroom Practices

Another Alternative for the Book Report [1]

Nancy Sparks, Teacher, Wichita High School Southeast, Wichita, Kansas

When my accelerated sophomore English class and I tired of the usual book report programs, we held a planning session one Friday to find a new approach. While the students enjoyed reading, they did not enjoy the routine pattern we had fallen into of giving book reviews. After several suggestions received only lukewarm enthusiasm, someone in the class proposed, somewhat facetiously, the idea of a "Book-of-the-Month Club," with the class to act as board of reviewers for the books reported on. The class, in complete agreement with the suggestion, set to work the remainder of the hour to draw up some guides for the program.

They first elected a planning committee to decide upon methods for organizing the club. The following Friday, the newly formed committee presented these proposals to the class:

1. Two days each month shall be devoted to the meetings of the club.
2. A list of suggested books shall be posted on a special bulletin board set aside for club news. (Any approved book list can be used.)
3. Each student shall read and present a book for class consideration. His presentation shall be in the form of a persuasive talk, not to exceed five minutes, to try to convince the class to vote for the book he read.
4. After all talks have been presented, the class shall vote by secret ballot for five books. The book receiving the most votes shall be the winner, with the four receiving the next highest number of votes the runners-up.
5. No book may be chosen the "Book-of-the-Month" more than

[1] Source: *English Journal,* November 1962. Reprinted with the permission of the National Council of Teachers of English and Nancy Sparks.

once. If a book places in the runner-up category, however, and the class feels it deserves another chance, someone else may read it and report on it.

6. A chairman shall be chosen to head a committee whose function will be to keep a record of every book reviewed and to count ballots.
7. A list of the winning books will be posted on the bulletin board. Each student will be required to read the top selection of the month sometime during the school year. The total number of books read during the year will be sixteen.
8. An art committee will be formed to design a book jacket for the winner of each month's meeting. These jackets will be placed on the club's bulletin board for display.
9. Eight monthly meetings will be held. The final meeting in May will be devoted to a discussion of the eight monthly winners. Because of this, it is essential that every student read the winning books as soon as possible.

Following the formulation of these rules, the class decided upon criteria for choosing and judging the books they would read, as well as methods of presentation. They agreed early that no more than a brief summary of the book should be given and that most of the talk should be devoted to persuading the class to vote for that book. Their talks were to point out the merits of the book, cite particularly effective passages, and discuss style as well as theme and content.

In the two years that I have used it, the program has met with great interest. It has been my experience that the students want their own copies of not only the top five books but some of the books not nominated, also. Since so many paperback editions are available today most students can afford their own copies. I have found, also, that they trade and share paperbacks so that no one is financially burdened.

The program, in my opinion, has several advantages. It first of all is something refreshing, different from a written report or a mimeographed form. It gives students an opportunity to examine books closely for their relative merit as "Book-of-the-Month." In fact, it is not uncommon for a student's sales talk to be "unpersuasive," to suggest to the class that the book does *not* deserve the nomination. One student even apologized to the class, saying, "I am almost embarrassed to talk about this book since I feel that it is probably elementary school-level reading. But I was in a hurry this month to find a book, and I didn't choose very carefully."

Perhaps, then, the program teaches students to evaluate their reading critically and to strive for a more mature level of reading. In addition, it guides them in effective oral expression before a group. But whatever its merits, the "Book-of-the-Month Club" above all motivates students to read and to enjoy what they read.

I Sing of the Paperback [2]

Sister M. Clarencia, C.C.V.I., Librarian,
Incarnate Word High School, San Antonio, Texas

To find a once hidebound librarian completely sold on paper-backs may be something of a rarity, but it is a fact. Indeed, it is much worse than that. Not only the librarian but the 450 girls in her school have become so paperback-conscious that they live and move, study and play, eat and drink in an atmosphere of paper-backs. Yet, the paperback has come into its own at Incarnate Word High School, San Antonio, Texas, and with it has come a thirst for reading, a new interest in studies, a marked eagerness for self-improvement, and a wholesome zest for life and living. In short, there is abundant evidence among the students of a veritable renaissance of learning, of a culture that is a palpable, flourish-ing, student-craved type of thing. And the cause of it all is neither the curriculum nor the teachers, nor the library nor the librarian, but the sprightly little paperback of which I sing.

To account for this renaissance of learning permit me to take you back to my first paperback experiment launched seven years ago at Incarnate Word Academy, St. Louis, Missouri. At that time I was not at all certain that the paperback was a worthy product to harbor much less to adopt within the sacred precincts of my fairly new high school library. What I did know was this: (1) that the girls liked paperbacks and that they bought them from the neighboring drug and department stores, and (2) that there existed a sufficient number of good ones for me to experiment with, sales-rack-wise, in my library as the drugstore did. Furthermore, I had

[2] Source: *The Catholic Educator*, March 1961. Reproduced by permis-sion of the publisher.

grown rather skeptical of the negative approach we, adult directors of youth, ordinarily employed; namely, that of contenting ourselves with denouncing the pornographic books, or of sponsoring, sporadically, a city-wide clean-up drive—neither of which activities produced any lasting remedy. A constructive approach, I reasoned, ought to search diligently for the good books, list and publicize them and, better still, make them available to students right within the school. And if the librarian is not "ordained" to espouse such a cause, then who in the school is?

QUALITY PAPERBACKS WERE MUSHROOMING

Like the majority of librarians seven years ago, I, too, was a hidebound one, passionately devoted to the solid worth of the hardbacks on my library shelves. With a certain amount of complacency I used to counsel myself and my fellow librarians to steer clear of the scrawny paperback. Facilely, I enumerated my litany of objections: lurid covers, weak bindings, objectionable matter, cheap paper, and small print. What sane librarian could succumb to these? And yet, as I scanned the bookracks in department stores, the book reviewing magazines in the library, and the paperback announcements in the library and English journals, I became aware of a new trend: quality paperbacks were mushrooming, and more and more girls were purchasing, reading, discussing, and enjoying them. This was the straw that broke the camel's back! I determined to experiment.

Fortified with such reflections I visited my favorite local bookstore and with the aid of its manager, a discerning bookman, I selected on credit several dozen paperbacks for my first experiment, with the understanding that I could return the unsold items, in due time. As soon as the books were delivered I displayed them on a floor wirerack. Centrally located and directly facing the main library entrance, the rack looked sprightly, colorful, inviting. Now that the stage was set, I sat back to watch the show. The first girl who entered walked directly to the rack, looked it over, examined one book, and then another. In a pleased and rather positive manner she picked up one and took it to the desk. Opening her pocketbook she announced challengingly, "Can I buy this now? It's about time you did something like this, Sister!" (That remark struck home. From then on I knew my course.) By way of the grapevine, the paperback news spread. Other eager readers dropped in that day and the next. By the third day there wasn't a paperback left.

At the suggestion of my student-assistants, I telephoned the local bookstore for a fresh batch. In addition, I hastily dispatched an order to Readers' Choice for an assortment of one hundred selected titles. As soon as these were delivered, up went the salesrack again, but this time a student-assistant made an announcement to that effect over the public address system for the benefit of those girls we had previously disappointed. These latter came running and breathless as students have come ever since in another library in response to a similar announcement: PAPERBACKS, PAPER-BACKS, A NEW FRESH BATCH! Thus began the paperback service which flourished in that library for a period of three years. It was not a service given daily but frequently: during Book Weeks, Book Fairs or Exhibits; during Lent and Retreat times, and prior to Christmas and summer vacations.

PERENNIALLY IN DEMAND

Although I kept no exact statistics of the paperbacks bought or sold during that first experiment, I know that the following titles were best-sellers and perennially in demand: Burnite's *Tips for Teens* (a $1.00 Bruce paperbound sold two hundred copies), Funk's *30 Days to a More Powerful Vocabulary,* Doyle's *Cana Is Forever,* Sheen's *Three to Get Married,* Merton's *Seven Storey Mountain* and *Seeds of Contemplation,* Frank's *The Diary of a Young Girl,* Timmerman's *The Perfect Joy of St. Francis,* Poage's *In Garments All Red,* Bronte's *Jane Eyre,* Austen's *Pride and Prejudice,* Connelly's *Mr. Blue,* Chesterton's *The Adventures of Father Brown,* Guareschi's *Don Camillo* books, Horgan's *Humble Powers,* Farrell's *The Looking Glass,* Spellman's *The Foundling,* Dolson's *We Shook the Family Tree,* and *Least of All Me.*

IMAGE BOOKS, TOO

All of the above-mentioned titles I stocked in dozens, but others, chiefly Image and Readers' Choice titles, I purchased singly or in duplicate by way of experimentation. Among paperbacks popular with the slow and reluctant readers were: *The Diary of a Young Girl, We Shook the Family Tree, The Foundling,* and the *Don Camillo,* and *Sue Barton* books, as well as a number of animal stories, light romances, and etiquette books. All freshmen—including the talented, slow, and reluctant readers—wanted a copy of *Tips for Teens* for their personal libraries. And every senior (the seniors were being given a very thorough course in marriage) purchased a copy of either *Cana Is Forever* or *Three to Get Married.*

When, in September 1957, I was transferred to Incarnate Word High School, San Antonio, Texas, I lost no time in introducing a similar paperback service there. And it is of this service—especially the manner of selecting books, the sources of supply, the mechanics of operation, the reading interests of the girls, and the over-all effects upon the entire community—that I wish to treat in the remainder of this article.

SELECTION OF BOOKS

I shall deal first with the selection of books, the most crucial point in the entire service.

The selection of books for any adolescent group is never an easy matter, but it can be made effective and fruitful for a given school by the sustained cooperative efforts of the librarian and the better-read teachers, especially those in the English and social studies areas. And thus it worked itself out in our school. In the beginning the librarian confined her selections to standard classics—ancient and modern—with which she was conversant, to the Image books that were suitable for high school students, and to the most highly recommended titles in the Readers' Choice catalog and the Teen Age Book Club offerings. But as the girls' interests expanded she perused other catalogs, chiefly *Paperbound Books in Print,* the Affiliated Publishers, Inc., catalog, and *A List of Acceptable Pocket-Size Books for Youth.* But since intelligent book selection is of primary importance in a book project that aims to improve the student's reading by permitting her to select freely from a rich assortment of quality books, we asked the aid of the English and social studies teachers who were eager to revise their reading lists and to screen certain adult or controversial items. The over-all policy of book selection on which we were unanimously agreed could be stated as follows: we wanted a major portion of books of solid literary worth, the adult rather than the adolescent novel, biographies of significant men and women that combined historical accuracy with literary merit, the better historical novels, and the well-written lives of the outstanding saints in Christendom. From the catalogs mentioned above, from the lists, from suggestions and recommendations of the faculty, we gradually compiled a basic working list that suited our students' curricular and personal needs.

SOURCES OF SUPPLY

From my sources of paperback supply, I have found three most satisfactory ones: (1) a local wholesale distributor; (2) Doubleday or the local Catholic bookstore for Image books suitable for high school students, and (3) Readers' Choice items to add spice and infinite variety to the service. And while all three of these give excellent service and liberal discounts for bulk orders, I have come to rely almost entirely on the regular, weekly Friday deliveries of the local distributor, who manifests a keen interest in the girls' lively response and pressing demands for more and better paperbacks.

To deal with a local wholesale distributor is a definite advantage for the librarian who has submitted her list of needed paperbacks several weeks or months in advance of the opening of school. Here's how we operate at present. A typical September consignment of books usually consists of a hundred titles or about a thousand copies. About twenty-five or fifty of these are attractively displayed on a desk-rack and on two display niches to the rear of the circulation desk. Titles are changed frequently—daily or weekly—depending on the interest, the demand, and the sales. The actual selling is carried on simultaneously with the various other library services rendered throughout the school day. While two trained desk-assistants usually help with the sales, the librarian is always close at hand to give reading guidance. It is this individual reading guidance that renders paperback service fruitful and that differentiates it from the casual type of service that must of necessity be given in a school bookstore. Furthermore, if reading guidance is one of the most important services rendered by the secondary school librarian, it is imperative that she take the paperback into her domain.

In our paperback set-up, Friday is generally a heavy sales day for two reasons: (1) it is delivery day, and (2) it is the beginning of a week-end. As many as seventy-five items have been sold on certain Fridays. Students are charged the retail price and the library nets a profit of 20 per cent. This profit goes into the paperback fund and is used to purchase the more costly paperbounds which the talented or gifted students demand. Bills are paid monthly after all unsold items for which there is no demand or further need are returned. Daily sales are very simply handled. Each student who purchases a book fills a one-line entry in our *Paperback Register*.

This register is left on the circulation desk at all times and each patron delights in entering her purchase. At the end of each month the library holds a paperback drawing and the student whose number is drawn may select a free paperback from those currently displayed. The paperback register provides us, further, with any additional statistics we need. From it we learn the number of sales per day, week, month, or year; which titles were best-sellers, which grades or groups are readers or non-readers, whether local "movies" or current television programs have influenced the sale of a particular book, which teachers are aware of the selections on hand, and which are influencing the reading habits of their students. What the register does not record are the individual requests of the students for books we have been unable to supply; yet these requests can at times be more revealing than their actual selections since the latter is limited to the titles stocked.

READING INTERESTS REVEALED

And what has this paperback service revealed about a girl's reading interests? That she likes fiction and romance? Yes, but that's not the total picture. Given ample pre-selected material, individual guidance, and freedom to make her own choices, a girl will select items from the entire field of literature: classics, ancient and modern, Greek and English plays, poetry, Shakespearean tragedies, short stories, and—if she is a senior high student—the adult rather than the adolescent novel. A sampling of best sellers spanning a seven-year period that takes into account the student population in two totally different high schools and areas should be convincing.

SAMPLE CHOICES

Here are the girls' own choices: Homer's *The Iliad, The Odyssey;* Plato's *Dialogues,* Dante's *Inferno,* Shakespeare's *Four Tragedies,* Dickens' *Oliver Twist, Great Expectations;* Scott's *Ivanhoe,* Bronte's *Jane Eyre,* Austen's *Pride and Prejudice,* Blackmore's *Lorna Doone,* Chesterton's *Ballad of the White Horse* and his *Adventures of Father Brown,* Le Fort's *Song at the Scaffold,* Noyes' *Secret of Pooduck Island,* Hawthorne's *Scarlet Letter,* Poe's *Tales and Verse,* O. Henry's *Short Stories,* Wilder's *The Bridge of San Luis Rey* and *Three Plays of Thornton Wilder,* James' *The Turn of the Screw* and *Daisy Miller,* Crane's *The Red Badge of Courage, Immortal Poems of the English Language, Pocket Book of Story Poems,*

Love Letters of Phyllis McGinley, Thompson's *A Pocketful of Poems,* Mauriac's *The Woman of the Pharisees,* Hemon's *Marie Chapdelaine,* S. M. C.'s *Brother Petroc's Return,* Pasternak's *Dr. Zhivago,* White's *A Watch in the Night,* Rostand's *Cyrano de Bergerac* and DeWohl's *The Quiet Light, Living Wood,* and *The Spear.*

INTERSPERSED TITLES

I have noticed, too, how every girl will, for her delight and refreshment, intersperse with the heavier books mentioned above short or humorous books such as: *Goodbye Mr. Chips, We Shook the Family Tree, Please Don't Eat the Daisies, Mr. Blue, Life with Father, Humble Powers, The Foundling, Trish,* and a *Sue Barton* or a *Don Camillo* item. Ninth graders have four favorites: *The Diary of a Young Girl, Jane Eyre, The Secret of Pooduck Island,* and Chute's *Stories from Shakespeare.* Books which the movies have popularized have a strong attraction for the slow, reluctant, and retarded reader: *Ben Hur, Quo Vadis, The Song of Bernadette, Embezzled Heaven*—she braves them all and then passes them to other members of her family: mother, father, brother, sister, each of whom is equally delighted with them.

GIRLS LIKE BIOGRAPHY

Girls like biography: they will read any interesting life of man or woman. The ninth grader seems to have a decided preference for queens, members of the royalty, and a whole army of saints, her favorites being: Maria Goretti, Joan of Arc, Thérèse of Lisieux, and Francis of Assisi. The senior high girl likes to read any great saint's life but she is quite curious about women in medicine and those foundresses who have zealously served humanity. Partly, but not wholly out of curiosity, almost every girl at all grade-levels will read one or more books about nuns, the convent, religious life. Paperbacks have popularized these: Sr. Catherine Thomas' *My Beloved,* Brinkley's *The Deliverance of Sister Cecilia,* Hulme's *The Nun's Story,* and *Least of All Me;* but the girls have many hardback favorites, such as Sr. Maria del Rey's *Bernie Becomes a Nun,* Sr. Mary Vianney's *And Nora Said Yes,* and Sr. Madeline De Frees' *In Springs of Silence.* Her other favorite books dealing with the lives or the times of saints are: *The Perfect Joy of St. Francis, In Garments All Red* (St. Maria Goretti), *The Quiet Light* (St. Thomas Aquinas), Farrow's *Damien the Leper,* Goodier's *Saints for Sinners,* Reynold's *St. Thomas More,* Beevers' *Storm of Glory* (St. Thérèse), Chesterton's *St. Thomas Aquinas* and *St. Francis of Assisi.* In fact, so avidly does the average girl seek this type of book that I feel justified in saying that after fiction—her favorite type of reading is a well-written life of a saint.

SEEKS SOLID SPIRITUAL FOOD

We feel that the modern girl seeks solid spiritual food and not pious readings. Here is the typical spiritual library that scores of the girls have built up as a result of school book fairs and exhibits as well as paperback service. In it you will find a copy of the New Testament or a complete Bible (the $1.00 Catholic Truth Society hardback is a favorite), a theology book such as Sheed's *Introduction to Theology,* or Farrell's *Way of Life;* a *Life of Christ* (Fouard's is giving way to Fulton Sheen's), a handy book for spiritual reading, such as Merton's *Seeds of Contemplation* or *No Man Is an Island,* two paperbacks which have been bestsellers in both schools. In addition the majority of the girls own a book for mental prayer, such as Paone's *Daily Bread;* a collected-lives of the saints and an individual life of a few other favorite saints. To this basic collection a senior usually adds a copy of *The Inferno, Seven Storey Mountain,* and *Cana Is Forever,* or *Three to Get Married,* all of which furnish excellent reading matter for discussion, reflection, and meditation, especially during retreat time.

A TOP FAVORITE, WITH LITERARY FLAVOR

This matter of a girl's delight in spiritual books deserves more than a passing comment. Perhaps the most valuable of all types of reading for the girl living in our mechanized, restive world is the profoundly religious book, especially that one which is true literature as well. To cite one example of a top-favorite with the girls, I give you *The Perfect Joy of St. Francis* by the Flemish poet, Felix Timmermans. Although this is not a definitive life but rather a delightful novel about St. Francis, it is a book that is passed from student to student within the walls of the classroom. Wherein lies the appeal of this book if not first in the literary flavor and secondly in the content itself? The book presents truth in such a fashion that a girl reads it primarily for the beauty of language and imagery, but while thus absorbed she is quietly contemplating its essential meaning and imbibing some of its spirituality into her own heart and soul. This is the type book a librarian should seek to provide: for, as with all great books, the more perfect the literary flavor, the more deep and lasting the spiritual significance. Girls don't argue with such a book: they simply become absorbed, lose themselves for a time in a spiritually satisfying world and come up, reluctantly, perhaps, but always refreshed. Spiritual classics, great poetry, and prayer have this in common: they possess a beauty and poignancy that stir the soul to desire eternal things. The sooner we introduce the adolescent girl to such a book the better, for the modern woman has need of great spiritual reserves to counteract the nervous ills and tensions that her generation is heir to.

What is the over-all effect of the paperback service on the students, their families, and the teachers in the school?

I have already stated that the paperback service has sparked the reading of all the students more effectively than any hardback has ever done. Students who never read are now reading; spontaneously, eagerly, joyously. Those who have always read are now reading more and better books. The slow student is learning to enjoy a book without pain or embarrassment.

In our school, moreover, the paperback service is a boon to the boarding students, especially to those who come from little country towns devoid of any library service whatever. Such students invest heavily in paperbacks prior to the Christmas and summer vacations.

The "Two-Bits" Book Club [3]

Stanley Solomon, English Teacher,
Linton High School, Schenectady, New York

My class studied paperbacks from first to last in a unit called "Paperback Bonanza." I approached the subject as a significant field of literature. This is the way I went about it:

GETTING READY

Books for Everyone (United World Films) provided the framework for later study. The film showed my youngsters how paperbacks are produced in quantity (over 90,000 a day); how they are widely distributed to some 110,000 outlets; how they have left a

---

[3] Source: Reprinted by permission from *Scholastic Teacher,* © 1961 by Scholastic Magazines, Inc.

deep impact on the culture of our times. We developed some questions we wanted to answer in our study.

A tackboard display featuring materials from Scholastic's Teen Age and Campus Book Clubs and Readers' Choice Service took shape. I placed near the door a revolving wire rack loaded with my own paperbacks and introduced the "Two-Bits Book Club": For 25 cents members received unlimited borrowing privileges with no strings attached (no book reports required). Money received was used to buy additional books. (Even youngsters not in the class joined the club. Every time they passed my room they saw the colorful rack through a glass panel.)

TYPES OF PAPERBACKS

The refuting of several disturbing misconceptions marked part of our study. Among them: that all paperbacks were of the black-listed kind; that all paperbacks were condensed versions of original books; that paperbacks were somehow too inviting to be "educational."

My students began to keep a list of new words that came up in our work. For example, why was *The Amazing Crime and Trial of Leopold and Loeb* listed under "Anthropology, Sociology and Psychology"? They found the answer after we heard a panel report on the above book, on Meyer Levin's *Compulsion,* and on the film of the same title. (This was an instance of comparing communication media, by the way.)

For another report I arranged the class in groups of four or five. Then I asked each group to study together one of the following classifications—Drama, Short Stories, American History, The World, Biography, The Arts and Science. Each member of the group used a different paperback title in the classification chosen. Finally, we heard group discussions in which each student explained why his book fell into its classification, what impressed him most about the book and a word or two on the design of the paperback.

OVERSEAS AMBASSADORS

It comes as a new idea to my youngsters that paperbacks serve as weapons in the deadly serious war of ideas that our country is waging. Both *Books for Everyone* and *Good Reading for the Millions* help explain how paperbacks present a picture of American ways of life abroad.

Each student read a paperback and then wrote a letter to the State Department suggesting why it should be stocked in our overseas libraries. We then pooled results so that several letters, each mentioning ten titles, were actually sent.

POPULAR TASTE

Paperbacks at three key locations in the city—a bookstore, a drugstore, a magazine dealer—were scrutinized by teams of students. Blurbs told them enough so that they could group books according to classifications previously mentioned. There was not exactly a *Walden* (at 50 cents) for every *Peyton Place,* but there was enough good reading to make evident the remarkable range and quality.

Ending this phase of our work, we more or less agreed that taste may be a question of reading what everyone else is reading, but it is also directly related to education, and to an awareness of the great range of subject matter available in paperback.

PAPERBACKS AS AN INDUSTRY

In this section of our work I aimed to tie together some of the things we had studied.

Some of the class wrote letters to a paperback publisher suggesting hardcover books they had read which might be published in paperback. They also included: specific audiences for the book; reasons why these audiences would be interested; evidence of popularity or value of the book; and a detailed description of what should appear on the cover.

Others elected to read a nonfiction paperback and then write why it should be selected as a high school text. They had to conceive at least five study questions for each chapter and comment on changes that would be necessary (such as easier vocabulary or illustrations).

A third group wrote a long paper with the title, "Good Reading for the Millions: The Age of Paperbacks." Included were: origins of paperbacks; rapid modern development; paperback publishers today, types available, with leading titles; availability of paperbacks; effects of paperbacks on the upraising and downgrading of taste; and finally, an evaluation of how far paperbacks go in entertaining and educating vast numbers of readers.

Soft-Covered Culture [4]

*Father James W. Sanders, S.J., English and Speech Department,
St. Ignatius High School, Chicago, Illinois*

Not often does a high school principal smile at being run down in the hallway by one of his students. But Rev. R. J. Knoepfle, S.J., principal of St. Ignatius High School, Chicago, Illinois, did just that one day last fall. The reason: the young man with whom he collided had been so absorbed in reading a paperback book while walking down the hall that he didn't see Fr. Knoepfle coming. The head-on collision gave final, jarring proof that the school's latest educational advancement—a paperback reading program for the entire student body—had succeeded beyond all expectations.

The program, briefly, is this: At the start of each year every boy is entitled to a total of from eight to ten paperback books. The money for these books comes from an activity fee paid with the tuition. The teacher of each English class chooses the books to be read. He orders the books and distributes them to the members of his class. Each boy reads a copy of the same book at the same time. At the end of a given period of time the teacher gives a test on the book to the entire class. After this there follows discussion of the book, frequently a composition on some aspect of plot or character development, and sometimes a study of the new vocabulary words.

The advantages of this program, as judged by the enthusiasm of both teachers and students, has been so overwhelming that school authorities feel it to be one of the greatest educational steps forward the school has made in many years.

FORCES STUDENTS TO READ

In the first place, the program forces students to read. This factor was the original motive in introducing the paperbacks. Previously each boy was required to read about eight books a year as part of his regular English course. The student selected these books from a list provided by the school. Usually he wrote a report on

[4] Source: *The Catholic Educator,* November 1959. Reproduced by permission of the publisher.

the book and received a grade as a result of the teacher's evaluation of this report.

The problem, however, was that many students made their book reports after reading a Classic Comic, a book digest, or another boy's book report. Reports were passed on from year to year and from boy to boy. Teachers knew this practice existed, but nothing could be done. Since each boy in a given class might be reading a different book, no common test could be given. Attempts at individual tests for each student proved rather unwieldy. Some boys, juniors and seniors, admitted they had never read an entire book in their high school careers, indeed, in their whole lives. There were, of course, some good readers; but the majority, even otherwise good students, did little reading. Too many other interests engaged their attention. Television and movies, in particular, took the place of good reading.

But with the advent of the paperback program, a teacher could give an objective exam on the book to be read, thus forcing the students to read it under pressure of failing that exam. In this respect, the program was successful from the start. Under pressure, the students did read their books.

LEADS TO ENJOYMENT

However, the "fringe benefits" of using paperbacks (as revealed in a questionnaire and in compositions about the program) soon pushed the original motive far into the background. Boys who had never read before took pride in having read a book. Further, reluctantly at first and then with growing enthusiasm, they began to answer their own arguments against reading: "I read the Classic Comic version; so why waste time reading the whole book?" "I saw the movie; so why read the book?" They began to realize that these arguments are not valid, that reading a Classic Comic does not bring them into intimate contact with the lives and problems of the characters, that they do not participate so fully in a comic or digest and therefore do not enjoy so much. They also began to realize that, while movies frequently add fresh insights, they always leave out far more than can be had from reading the book.

This new-found joy in reading generated so much enthusiasm that by the end of the first experimental year a questionnaire revealed that only 2.5 per cent of the student body (twenty-five out of a thousand boys) disliked the program. Oddly enough, most of the dissenters were talented boys who had already been good readers.

They objected to being told what to read. This objection had been foreseen by members of the English department, and had caused some concern.

ALLOWS CLASS DISCUSSION

But this difficulty, too, has worked itself out naturally during the second year of the program, largely as a result of what most English teachers now consider the greatest single advantage of the program: organized class discussion on the books read. Students who already had a solid habit of reading now readily admit that class discussion, made possible only by the fact that each member of the class has read the same book, has greatly enhanced their power to understand and appreciate the books read. The opportunity for class discussion also makes it possible for teachers to choose more mature books and to include books which might be objectionable without adequate explanation. Teachers can bring out values embodied in the books, and students can share one another's insights.

Thus, students who did not read before find themselves reading, enjoying, and understanding the best of the world's literature; students who were already readers are reading better books and understanding and appreciating them more fully.

ENCOURAGES FURTHER READING

Further evidence for the success of the program might be seen in the fact that many classes are asking to read more than their quota. In the second year of the program, by Christmas time, several classes had read all the books paid for by the year's activity fee, then voted unanimously to finance their own reading program for the second semester. These classes have read from twenty to twenty-five books in the course of a single school year (at a cost of about 3.5 cents a day). Several teachers have also instituted paperback lending library services, collecting a series of softcover books not given to the class as a whole, then lending these to individual students for extra reading and extra credit. By popular request the school's bookstore has also stocked a line of paperbacks not used in the regular reading program. Also by request of students, some teachers have given their classes lists of suggested paperback reading for the summer months and for future life.

This, of course, suggests another unforeseen "fringe benefit" of the program: Many students have begun their own libraries. They carefully guard and save the books from the reading program itself and add books of their own choice to this collection as their finances permit. They seem to be taken by the joy of possession; and the attractive appearance of most paperback books adds to this joy. While these books may not be so durable as hard covers, if handled properly they do last, and provide an excellent opportunity to amass an inexpensive collection of the world's best literature.

The handy pocket size of these books has added another advantage. Teachers have found that almost the normal load of ordinary English homework—composition, grammar, vocabulary—can still be given, one reason being that most students find the reading enjoyable, and, therefore, not to be classified strictly as homework. Also, students carry their books with them, reading at odd moments of the day otherwise wasted. It is a common sight all year to see boys in the cafeteria reading pocket books as they munch sandwiches. Since most St. Ignatius students travel considerable distances to school, many have developed the habit of reading on the bus. Some of the more eager have even been seen pulling out pocket books between halves of athletic contests. Finally, and not so desirable, complaints have come from teachers of other subjects who found boys reading English class pocket books during history, math, or language classes.

These teachers have countered, however, by instituting modified reading programs of their own. Many teachers in the history department now assign paperback books to supplement the text. In the language departments also, boys are reading the classics of Greek, Roman, and Russian literature to supplement their textual studies.

IMPROVES WRITING

As a result of the vast increase in the quality and quantity of the students' reading, English teachers have also noticed a marked improvement in writing. A sense of good English style, a feeling for idiom, a wider range of vocabulary seem to come as natural byproducts of good reading. Some teachers have made explicit attempts to correlate the reading program with other objectives of the English course: encouraging the underlining (another advantage of the paperback) and looking up of new words; making up lists of difficult words taken from each book read and requiring the students to know them; selecting striking passages for imitation exercises in writing; assigning compositions on character study, evaluation, and comparison of books read.

The program as a whole has grown in popularity among the students to the point where the only objections ever raised are to selections of individual books sometimes made by individual teachers. In general, teachers have tried to select books combining high entertainment value with solid literary worth. The choices in some instances have not been well made, but experience is gradually ironing out these difficulties.

As the program progresses, the chairman of the English department is compiling a list of available and approved paperback books, a separate list for each of the four years. (A semi-annual publication, *Paperbound Books in Print,* from R. R. Bowker, makes this task considerably easier.) Each teacher makes his selections from this list.

The first consideration in approving books has been to eliminate any book judged to be harmful to faith or morals. This has sometimes necessitated the exclusion of otherwise good books printed with suggestive, lurid, and even indecent covers, a practice which the paperback industry is, happily, gradually growing out of.

The lists correspond to the objectives of the standard literature anthology textbooks still used in the school's English courses: English literature in fourth year; American literature in third year; training in appreciation in second year; enjoyment in first year. Thus, third and fourth year teachers have priority on the classics of American and English literature, respectively. Within each year, of course, the choice of books depends upon the level of each class. Since all classes are grouped homogeneously according to natural talent and actual achievement, a more satisfactory selection of books on a class-wide basis can be made.

As should be evident from the following book lists, selections have been made heavily from the more widely reputed authors. Teachers have found that with the help of class lectures or discussions before, during, and/or after the reading of these more mature books, the majority of students can and do find them enjoyable, understandable, and profitable. Through these lectures and discussions teachers can also settle moral and ethical problems arising in certain books, problems which might otherwise render these books undesirable for the ordinary teen-ager.

SAMPLING FROM THE LIST

This list does not include all books used in the program, but is meant to afford a generous sampling of those used in various years. Books marked with an asterisk have been found well suited for the better students only; those unmarked are thought to be suited for all.

First year: *Kon Tiki,* Heyerdahl; *Beau Geste,* Wren; *Treasure Island,* Stevenson; *Tom Sawyer,* Twain; *Memoirs of Sherlock Holmes,* Doyle; *A Night to Remember,* Lord; *Hiroshima,* Hersey; *Don Camillo and His Flock,* Guareschi; *The Light in the Forest,* Richter; *Shane,* Schaefer; *Old Yeller,* Gipson; *The Adventures of Captain David Grief,* London; *Saint Among the Hurons,** Talbot; *Damien the Leper,** Farrow; *Ivanhoe,** Scott.

Second year: *Great Short Stories of Robert Louis Stevenson;** *Huckleberry Finn,* Twain; *Mutiny on the Bounty* and *The Hurricane,* Nordhoff and Hall; *Robinson Crusoe,** Defoe; *David Copperfield,** Dickens; *Goodbye Mr. Chips,* Hilton; *The Black Arrow,* Stevenson; *Captain from Connecticut,* Forester; *The Last of the Mohicans,** Cooper. Second year reading can also be filled out, especially for the poorer readers, by books skipped in first year. While it is true that freshmen and sophomores generally favor fast moving action stories, teachers have found that some of the more solid but slower moving works mentioned above can safely and profitably be sandwiched in between the more melodramatic ones.

Third year: *The Scarlet Letter,* Hawthorne; *Moby Dick,* Melville; *Great Tales and Poems of Edgar Allan Poe; The Virginian,* Wister; *The Red Badge of Courage,* Crane; *The Turn of the Screw* and *Daisy Miller,** James; *Dodsworth,* Lewis; *The Sea Wolf,* London; *The Bridge of San Luis Rey,* Wilder; *The Late George Apley * or *Point of No Return,** Marquand; *The Pearl,* Steinbeck; *The Last Hurrah,* O'Connor; *Mr. Blue,* Connolly; *Great American Short Stories,** Stegner, Ed.; *The Sea Around Us,** Carson (for training in good natural science reading); *Thank you, Mr. Moto,* Marquand; *Magnificent Obsession,* Douglas; *Saint Among the Hurons,* Talbot.

Fourth year: *Jane Eyre,* Charlotte Bronte; *Rebecca,* DuMaurier; *William Shakespeare, Five Plays,* Rinehart ed.; *Oliver Twist,* Dickens; *Lord Jim,* Conrad; *South Sea Stories,* Maugham; *Beowulf; Gulliver's Travels,* Swift; *Tale of Two Cities,* Dickens; *Great Expectations,* Dickens; *Lost Horizon,* Hilton; *The Invisible Man,*

Wells; *The Citadel*, Cronin. In addition to many of the above, fourth year advanced placement students read: *St. Francis of Assisi* and *St. Thomas Aquinas*, Chesterton; *Victory*, Conrad; *The Mill on the Floss*, Eliot; *The Picture of Dorian Grey*, Wilde; *Pride and Prejudice*, Austen; *The Return of the Native*, Hardy; *Great English and American Essays*, Rinehart ed.; *Eight Great Comedies; Johnson and Boswell Reader*.

LESS ADVANCED STUDENTS

Less advanced students of all years read the easier of the works mentioned above, fill in with works skipped in the earlier years, and in some cases add lower level but good reading mysteries, westerns, war stories, or human interest stories: *The Babe Ruth Story*, Considine; *Away All Boats*, Dodson; *The A.B.C. Murders, The Murder of Roger Ackroyd, Witness for the Prosecution, Hickory Dickory Death, Poirot Loses a Client*, Agatha Christie; *The Wright Brothers*, Kelly; *They Fought for the Sky*, Reynolds; *F.B.I. Story*, Whitehead; *The Amazing Adventures of Father Brown*, Chesterton; *Fear Strikes Out*, Piersall; *Submarine*, Beach.

FOR HISTORY CLASSES; LANGUAGES, TOO

History: The history department's paperback program is still in the first stages of development. Books now in use are: First Year: *Christopher Columbus, Mariner*, Morison; *Napoleon*, Ludwig. Second Year: *Only Yesterday*, Allen; *John Adams and the American Revolution*, Bowen; *The Uprooted*, Handlin; *A Stillness at Appomattox*, Catton. Advanced Placement: *American History after 1865*, Billington; *The American Political Tradition*, Hofstadter; *Social Darwinism in American Thought*, Hofstadter.

Languages: Students of Latin read: *History of Rome*, Hadas; *Cicero and the Roman Republic*, Cowell; *Aeneid*, Vergil; *Imperial Rome*, Tacitus; *Confessions of St. Augustine; Roman Readings*, Grant, Ed. Students of Greek read: *Histories*, Herodotus; *Peloponnesian Wars*, Thucydides; *Seven Greek Plays; Odyssey* and *Iliad*, Homer. Students of a voluntary course in Russian language and culture read: *War and Peace*, Tolstoy; *Crime and Punishment*, Dostoevski; *The Portable Chekhov*, Yarmolinsky, Ed.; *Lenin*, Shub; *The Russian Revolution of 1917*.

The fact that high school students are reading, enjoying, and appreciating books like those mentioned above, and asking for more of them, seems to prove beyond doubt that the average high schooler is capable of good reading if he can be brought into contact with it. The wealth of highest caliber literature at the lowest possible prices and in the most convenient and persuasive form made available by a paperback reading program can, perhaps, be the most successful means of establishing that contact, a contact destined to develop a solid appreciation of the finest in the world's culture.

Team Teaching and the English Program [5]

John J. Rouse, Supervisor of Language Arts,
Hicksville Senior High School, Hicksville, New York

If only, one laments—and I am a lamenter of long standing—the educational innovations of recent years would be used for education. Take team teaching. Rather than being used for the curricular improvements it might effect, it is too often exploited for its publicity value. The concept makes available a whole vocabulary of up-to-date phrases with which to impress the taxpayer: "flexible grouping," "learning from a master teacher," "large-group instruction," "freeing the teacher from routine tasks," and, best of all, "study in depth." With a scheduling arrangement called "team teaching" a school can be modern without effort.

One illustration of how paperbacks can be used in team teaching is provided by the program developed for the English department of the Hicksville Senior High School in the Town of Oyster Bay, Long Island. Although the units that have been taught are not all of the same kind, the one I will describe here indicates the central place paperbacks have in the program.

The first unit taught by the tenth grade team this year used *Twenty Grand Short Stories* (Bantam, 50 cents), edited by Ernestine Taggard, as the basic text. The working title for this unit was "Exploring Character and Human Relationships." Titles for units seem always to promise too much or too little, and I'm afraid this one is no exception. It even has a clinical sound. Tenth graders exploring character and human relationships, indeed! (*Understanding the Universe* was the title of a ninth-grade science book I once studied, and even then I thought the author showed a certain reck-

[5] Source: *School Paperback Journal,* April 1965. Reprinted by permission of the publisher.

less daring. Today one might promise the moon, but the whole universe—?) However, what matters is that a direction be found for approaching the material, one rich in possibilities. This title served us well.

The first lesson was given in the lecture room, to which each of the six teachers involved sent half her class. It was the team leader's responsibility to begin the unit with these 96 students and arouse their interest in the work to come. Since this lesson provides a good example of the typical "lecture," I will describe it in some detail.

The teacher began by remarking that to most people psychology is a fascinating subject. We are anxious to know what makes other people "tick" and also, by gaining insight into others, we hope to understand ourselves better. In order to stimulate thought on the question of why people behave as they do, the teacher read from an article on vandalism published in a local newspaper, and asked the students for their explanations of the vandals' behavior. Another article used in the same way was Joseph Lelyveld's "The Paradoxical Case of the Affluent Delinquent," *New York Times Magazine* of October 4, 1964.

The teacher then went on to raise such questions as these: "Haven't we all done something, and then afterward wondered why?" "Haven't we all done things we knew we shouldn't, things we knew might even hurt us? Why?" He then presented several examples of behavior from his own observations and asked for possible explanations.

After this brief discussion (the lectures are somewhat informal, but of course such a large group makes extended discussion impossible), the teacher was sure the students were engaged with the subject, and asked them to read a story with him: "Let's see what you make of this story. Why does the boy in it, Bottles Barton, act as he does?" Since the story, Michael Fessier's "That's What Happened to Me," lends itself very well to oral presentation, the teacher read it aloud as the students followed in books distributed earlier.[a] The possible motivations for the boy's behavior were then discussed, with both teacher and students pointing out clues in the text of the story.

By this time the students were ready for the first assignments. For the next lesson, when they would return to their regular teachers for a small-class session, they were asked to read Marjorie

[a] This story is in Macmillan's paperback volume, *Short Story I* ($1.12).

Rawlings' story, "A Mother in Mannville," and decide why the two characters behave as they do. For the next lecture (lesson three) each student was to describe in two or three sentences an incident that had happened to him, or that he had observed, which involved behavior he was unable to understand or explain at the time.

Each student left the lecture room with a copy of *Twenty Grand Short Stories* and, we hope, the knowledge that he was about to have some interesting experiences. Subsequent lectures further developed the problems of character and behavior presented in the stories, and related them to the world at large. The lecturer, of course, is able to collect and use material not ordinarily available to all the six teachers with whom he works. This includes newspaper clippings, articles, pictures, recordings, and films.

The small-class sessions, none larger than eighteen students, allow for much more individual expression than is possible in the over-large English classes that are so common. In the small classes there is time for teacher and students to explore the assigned stories thoroughly. There is also time for the teacher to help students with their writing. The simple writing assignment given during the first lecture period was the beginning of a developmental writing program. The more difficult writing problems were scheduled for every fifth lesson, when no lecture was given and the students went to the classrooms. There, with the help of the small-class teacher, they worked on the writing problem for which the lecturer and their teacher had been preparing them during the week.

Once such a unit is well underway and the students have a body of reading in common, then other material can be introduced. The various small classes can each read a different work—selected, however, because it further illuminates the subject of the unit. This prepares the way for reports and panel discussions before the lecture group. Also, titles can be selected with the interests and ability level of a particular small class in mind. Paperback titles suitable for use with this unit include Helen Keller's *The Story of my Life* (Dell, 50 cents), Stephen Crane's *The Red Badge of Courage* (several editions available), Harper Lee's *To Kill a Mockingbird* (Popular, 60 cents), F. Scott Fitzgerald's *The Great Gatsby* (Scribner's, $1.25), H. G. Felsen's *Crash Club* (Bantam, 45 cents), and John Steinbeck's *The Pearl* (Bantam, 45 cents).

Given the great number of teachable books now available as paperbacks, the possibilities of developing such projects as the one described here are endless. Three such units have been developed so far for the English department of the Hicksville Senior High School, and more are planned. Team teaching need not be merely a mechanical rearrangement of teachers and children. It can, in fact, through the use of paperbacks, offer unusual opportunities for reforming and revitalizing the English curriculum.

You Can Individualize Your Reading Program, Too [6]

Mary Ann Daniel, Fifth-grade Teacher

Individualized reading—here at last was a method which could cope with the wide range of reading abilities within my classroom. The best way to meet individual differences is to deal with them individually. Now, my classroom was going to be different. Reading was going to be fun!

As I gazed at the thirty-six faces—some eager, some apprehensive—on the first day of school, I wondered if my plan would succeed. It sounded perfect in every article I had read. But thirty-six fifth-grade youngsters! My school district believes in grouping for reading. Almost every classroom in our eleven elementary schools has three reading groups. The size of my class and the policy of the school district would certainly encourage the "old-fashioned" grouping.

But I was determined to work out a plan to combine group and individualized reading. First I checked the reading ability of all the children, both for grouping and for my records for individualized reading. Each child read a paragraph from a story and we talked about it briefly. We also talked of how they felt about reading in general. It was both amazing and discouraging to discover the number of children who responded, "I hate it; I can't read."

We had our regular reading groups. Gradually I worked out a plan—with the top group first. One day a week, during a reading period, they could read any book they selected. I checked what they read individually that day. The other two groups responded, as I hoped they would, by demanding to know why they also

[6] Source: *English Journal,* November 1956. Reprinted with the permission of the National Council of Teachers of English and Mary Ann Daniel.

couldn't read a book of their own choice. Soon everyone was making his own selection from our room library.

From there it was easy to guide the children into forming a book club. The first undertaking was a book exchange. Books were brought from home—all excellent ones. One child brought in a comic book, and the youngsters themselves decided they didn't want any more! The first president of the club, a capable girl, planned programs for book quizzes, classifying the library shelves (the fifth-grade star football player took charge of this task), and getting others interested in reading. The children decided to present book reviews at least once a week. At first our book reviews were merely short résumés. The more imaginative youngsters later presented drawings, puppet shows, and short plays, all during a regular reading period or in the afternoon. Our workbook exercises still got done, however!

Reading periods, when we had the individualized program, ran forty to sixty minutes. During that time I saw children individually —volunteers first. We talked about what happened in the book, discussed the characters and their actions, made predictions of what was to come, and read a paragraph orally. Any difficulties the child had were noted, and worked on later. If there was a common problem for five or six youngsters, we went over it together. Individual problems were taken care of individually without wasting the time of the group.

The children kept diaries of the books they read. They could not understand, at first, that it was permissible to say they did not like a book. They all thought they had to say they liked every book!

After reading several books, the children were encouraged to write their own stories. These were put into book form—bound and illustrated—instead of just written on "good penmanship paper." These were kept in a conspicuous place available at all times. What could thrill a child more than to see someone reading his bound book?

The time allotted for book reporting is most valuable. It is amazing to watch the change and improvement. At first all reports seemed to follow the same pattern: "This book was about . . . . If you want to know what happened read it." An original presentation by just one youngster was all that was needed. Soon we had radio reporters, plays, pictures, drawings on the blackboard, *papier-maché* puppets, string puppets, and book reviews written in our classroom newspaper. The more creative the presentation, the more irresistible the book became to the other youngsters.

This creativeness carried over to the regular group which I still had three days a week. Here, too, we did more dramatization. We felt freer to select stories in the basic reader that had a particular interest instead of reading from the first story to the last in sequence. The children felt much freer to come to me for assistance. Those who finished first now worked on their book diaries or methods of presenting books.

As I have watched this reading program develop, I have been most pleased. It has enabled me to know more about each child. I have been able to give more worthwhile individual and group help. As the children read more, they become more skilled in selecting books that they understand and that are well-written. Weaker pupils are not embarrassed to select easier books; superior readers are not held back. Because the slower readers choose books they can read, they soon develop confidence. Their whole attitude towards reading is changed. In the individualized program the children want to read; the more they read, the greater degree of success they feel in all their school work.

Paperbacks for Advanced Students

Honors Reading Program in a Senior High School [1]

Jane K. Billings, Library Supervisor, and Joan A. Paulson, Chairman,
English Department, Clintonville High School, Clintonville, Wisconsin

The Honors Reading Program was initiated to motivate the academically talented students to read better quality literature and to help them enjoy doing so. How often had we heard a college freshman say, "But why didn't you *make* me read more and better books when I was in high school?" That college student had forgotten the image of himself in high school; he placed sports, clubs, job, and social life before academic achievement.

In 1958 we decided to launch a project beyond the regular curriculum: an honors reading program for a group of ten students. First we established certain criteria for selection: intellectual and reading abilities, the recommendation of former teachers, and the student's ability to get along with the others, i.e., the ability to disagree with, but respect the opinions of fellow students and teachers. Then we discussed the proposal with the high school principal and the superintendent of schools. From the superintendent we asked neither time nor funds, for this was an experiment, and we were willing to take the full responsibility for it—rise or fall. (Now, however, the school purchases our copies of the paperbacks and allocates a fund which we may use for special purposes. Last year we took the senior group to see a play at a nearby college.)

Having obtained administrative approval, we selected our pilot group of ten students for a year's project. This project now involves two groups, each one selected in the fall of the junior year and continued through the senior year. Next we wrote a letter to the parents of the selected students, asking them to meet with us to discuss the proposed program. All students were represented by their mothers and some by both parents. The parents were told that the program would stress quality of literature, not quantity, and that it would not be additional work but in lieu of certain assignments

[1] Source: *English Journal*, May 1965. Reprinted with the permission of the National Council of Teachers of English and Jane K. Billings and Joan A. Paulson.

140

in English. Further, we explained the criteria by which the students had been chosen.

Since we felt that these students should be encouraged to own books and to underline and to mark comments and meaningful passages in their books, we recommended that each student purchase his own paperback copy, and the parents agreed to pay for the books. The parents offered to take turns in providing refreshments for each meeting, because we found sociability and informality prevailed more readily when cookies were available.

The parents were also told how literary selections would be chosen for group reading, that the books might be somewhat more "worldly" than the literature they had read at that age. At this point they had an opportunity to ask questions and to let us know, whether in the light of what they had been told, they wanted their child to be included. They all did.

The next step was to confer with each student individually (we now do this as a group), to explain the program as we did for the parents, and to ask the student if he were interested in participating. We made it clear that should he not want to participate, it would make no difference in our relationships or feelings toward him. In the past six years only one student has not wanted to participate, because he "needed the time for basketball."

After explaining the proposed program to our first group, we considered the selection of materials. We formulated our Pilot Reading Project List; this list contained both those books which we felt would be challenging to college-bound high school students and those which we felt any well-read high school student would have read previously; we suggested those missed would make good summer reading. The selection of books for this list was based on several sources.

Typically, the group includes the leaders and the non-leaders, a generous representation of athletes along with boys who dislike physical education, the normally quiet youngsters as well as the vocal type. The groups have been extremely heterogeneous socially, economically, and religiously and thus provide a valuable experience for the students, each of whom brings another point of view to the discussion. In several cases tolerance, understanding, and friendships have developed.

The library or lounge has appeared to be the most convenient place to meet, where we sit around a long table with cookies in the center and discuss the books. Each group decides at one meeting the date and time of the following meeting; the most popular meeting time appears to be 7:30 in the evening. Meetings before and immediately after school are not satisfactory. Discussions usually last about one and one-half hours, but occasionally we have to draw the meeting to a close after two and one-half to three hours. Although we meet about once a month, the schedule is kept flexible because of set school and interschool activities.

Early in this project we experimented with the discussion of several books at a meeting, but experience has shown us that even two books by one author are too many. We tried having half of the group read *The Mayor of Casterbridge* and the other half read *The Return of the Native*. This was not successful, because one half did not know what the other half was talking about. Consequently, each student reads his own paperback copy of one title in preparation for a meeting.

At each session a leader volunteers or is elected to serve at the next meeting. We discuss the responsibilities of the leader carefully with the group, so there is no doubt regarding what we expect. The leader has a greater responsibility to do research in literary criticism and on the author's background than have the other members of the group. In advance he formulates good discussion questions. An additional responsibility is to bring all members into the discussion, to keep the group on the subject, and to curb those who are verbose.

Although we hold these meetings on an informal basis, each member has obligations. Needless to say, everyone must complete the book, think it through, find out what literary critics have said about it, express his opinions, and help to bring out the opinions of others.

Students are encouraged to think for themselves, but this does not preclude disagreement with others (arguments do become heated), so long as they understand the book and hold one another in mutual respect. This same mutual respect exists on a teacher-pupil relationship. We have never found that the students stepped over that fine line of familiarity toward us.

A noticeable pattern of group growth is discernible in the two years that we work with the students. As juniors, looking for details and being too literal in an interpretation of the story, they tend to obliterate any overall understanding. By the time they are seniors, they comprehend the story as a whole. The group has taken shape; somehow they seem to have developed in such a way that we can enjoy discussions on a more mature level. For several years we thought that only the advisors were aware of this, but we learned that by the time they were seniors, they were proud of the way they had learned to think and respond. As seniors they learned not only to value their own opinions, but also those of other students and the opinions of literary critics. They feel that they have "learned to think more deeply," and are less certain that they are right.

Since 1958, when the project started, many new materials have become available. Some of those we use are:

1. *Books For You*—"A Reading List for Senior High School Students," N.C.T.E.
2. "Ceilings Unlimited," a bibliography of bibliographies alphabetically listing books which appeared on several lists for the college-bound.
3. "Horizons Unlimited," Indiana Council of Teachers of English and the N.C.T.E.
4. "Outstanding Biographies for College-bound Students," A.L.A. —Young Adult Services Division.
5. "Outstanding Fiction for College-bound Students," A.L.A.— Young Adult Services Division.
6. "Planned Reading for the College-bound Student," prepared by Wisconsin Improvement Program, Summer, 1960, and compiled and now used by Madison (Wis.) Public Schools.
7. "Preparing for College," which we prepared as a result of a survey; in the summer of 1960, we wrote to the chairmen of English Departments in eighteen colleges and universities throughout the country and asked them to list the ten books they would most like their incoming freshmen to have read.
8. "Reading List for College-bound Students," compiled by Wisconsin Council of Teachers of English.
9. "Suggested Reading List," prepared by the Academic Affairs Committee of the Wisconsin Student Association of the University of Wisconsin.

We use these many lists as a rudder not an anchor. There are other things which we must take into consideration in the selection of materials. For example, some books lend themselves to discussion more readily than others. We have learned from experience that a group composed of a somewhat equal number of boys and girls works best; therefore, we are concerned with the reading interests of both sexes.

As sponsors of these groups, we feel that we have many responsibilities. We find that we read four books to each one the students read; we do this not only to make sure the books they choose are those which lend themselves to discussion, but also to give us adequate background. We realize that a further obligation to these young people is not only to lead them to the best materials in literary criticism, but also to teach them to think critically. We feel that we have also the responsibility of giving the parents an appraisal of their child's growth. At the end of each school year we send a letter to the parents evaluating the growth of the group, as well as the progress made by their son or daughter. For those students who have missed reading significant books earlier, we ask their parents to encourage summer reading to include these titles.

Besides the many obligations to our students and their parents, we have an obligation to each other—that of displaying a kind of intellectual honesty; we must respect one another's opinions, share opinions and materials, discuss books, agree or disagree on points, and be willing to search for answers; in short, cosponsors of groups of these kinds must cooperate in the strictest and best sense of the word. There must be no idea of competition with each other. This program is an example of interdepartmental cooperation attempting to bring together and to use the best materials of both departments.

Teaching Research Techniques with Paperbacks [2]

David E. Newton, Chemistry Instructor at
Ottawa Hills High School, Battle Creek, Michigan

During the academic year 1964–65, a pilot course in science is being offered at Ottawa Hills High School, Grand Rapids, Michigan. The course, entitled "Foundations of Science," deals with the history, philosophy, and methodology of science. Thirty-five students (thirty sophomores and five freshmen) have been selected from about a hundred volunteer applicants for the course. Its primary objectives are to help students understand the nature of science and to develop an appreciation of the way in which scientists work.

[2] Source: *School Paperback Journal,* February 1965. Reprinted by permission of the publisher.

The "Foundations of Science" curriculum consists of two major portions, classroom work and laboratory exercises. The basis of the classroom work is an analysis of three major problems of historic interest in science: (1) motion and the structure of the universe, (2) the structure of matter, and (3) physical and organic evolution. While much of the laboratory work is related directly to the topics being considered in the classroom (e.g.: Galileo's experiments on the pendulum and on free fall were both repeated), another portion of the lab work is more general in nature, dealing with the methods and techniques of science. A large portion of this work is open-ended, providing students with an opportunity to "practice" problem-solving through experimentation.

TEAM TEACHING

One of the significant characteristics of the FOS course is its conscious attempt to employ the latest and most efficient methods of teaching. Elements of team teaching are involved in the use of staff members from the following departments: biology, physics, chemistry, earth science, English, social studies, and mathematics. Class time deviates from the usual 55 minute daily class sessions and is blocked, instead, in two-hour sessions meeting three days a week. Programmed units are used to supplement basic class material for those students with varying backgrounds. Regular work within the classroom is centered almost entirely around individual research, i.e. *student* activity, rather than *teacher* activity. A visitor to the FOS classroom would note that it is the students, and not the teachers, who are responsible for whatever is going on.

STUDENT PARTICIPATION

Thus, individual and group reports (e.g. "mock" reports to scientific academies), group discussions, debates (e.g. between Ptolemaists and Copernicans), student demonstrations, individual and group projects, original dramatization (e.g. "The Court Alchemist"), written exercises of many types—these forms of direct student participation are utilized to enable students to develop a variety of skills in researching, recording, and reporting data. Obviously, the demands of such a course for reference materials are considerable. To meet these demands, a large shelf of paperback books has been assembled for reference purposes. It is this extensive use of paperback books with which this article is concerned.

One of the first problems encountered in determining the teaching methods of the FOS course was the selection of a textbook. It became apparent, after a fairly thorough search, that no single book would satisfy the innumerable demands which the FOS course created. As a result, it was the consensus of the planning committee that a variety of paperback books would be selected to serve as a class library, a reference shelf from which all students could draw. The final decision to rely on paperbacks was based on six major considerations, as follows:

WHY PAPERBACKS?

1. Paperbacks permit one to adapt books to the course and not, as is so often the case, the course to a book. Most teachers have seen too many examples of the alternative. The selection of a single text is sometimes the most deadening and disastrous event to occur within a course. From that time on, the lesson plans become, "read and answer from the textbook." Beyond this obvious consideration, it was clear that no single book or even small number of books adequately covered the topics to be included in the FOS course.

2. Paperbacks provide a more thorough and more adaptable collection of references on specialized topics. When restricted to a single, pre-selected textbook, an instructor is always forced to search for additional resource materials and books on topics which he wishes to cover, but which are not included in great detail in the single text. This point was of particular importance in the FOS course since such an unusual collection of topics was to be considered. Thus, paperbacks have made it possible for us to pursue in considerable detail such esoteric topics as Arabic science and culture, alchemy, and the phlogiston theory in the paperbacks *The Arabs* (Hitti, Gateway, 95 cents), *The Alchemists* (Taylor, Collier, 95 cents), and *Case History of the Phlogiston Theory* (Conant, et al., Harvard, $1.00). Such work would have been either very shallow or actually impossible using a single reference.

The somewhat unusual combination of topics in FOS would also have proved to be awkward without the availability of paperbacks. It is strange that there are so very few history of science books which do a really adequate job in dealing with both physical and biological sciences for high school students. Mason's *History of the Sciences* (Collier, $1.95) is, perhaps, the outstanding exception. The detailed study of the impact of science on culture and vice versa, a major objective of the course, would also have proved to be an enormous problem with only a single book available.

3. Paperbacks permit an instructor to give a wider variety of "extra" assignments. The use of a number of reference books on satellite topics (e.g., Standen's *Science is a Sacred Cow,* Everyman, $1.15) seemed to be desirable, but beyond the means of the course's budget if they had to be purchased as hardcover books. As it is, an adequate number of these books is now available in paperback editions.

4. Paperbacks allow greater use of primary references. It was felt by the planning committee that extensive reading of primary references was desirable. For example, one of the major resources in the unit on motion and astronomy should be, it was felt, the original treatise by Galileo on *Two New Sciences.* The purchase of such books *in addition to* the standard references would have been economically impossible. Now, students may go directly to original sources by referring to any one of the many Dover editions of complete works or by referring to a collection such as the *Readings in the Literature of Science* edited by Dampier (Torchbooks, $1.50).

An understanding of these source materials may be developed by additional reference to various analytical commentaries which are also available as paperbacks: *Origins of Modern Science* (Butterfield, Macmillan, $1.25), *Metaphysical Foundations of Modern Science* (Burtt, Anchor, 95 cents), *Birth of a New Physics* (Cohen, Anchor, 95 cents), and *The Restless Atom* (Romer, Anchor, 95 cents) are examples.

5. Paperbacks provide a greater opportunity for the development of research techniques. One of the major objectives of the course, the improvement of students' abilities to carry on library research, is difficult without a fairly extensive number of books on hand. Familiarity with a single book or even a small number of books is no substitute for the opportunity of working with dozens of different kinds of books, learning the wide variety of books with which one comes into contact in serious library research. With a single textbook, the students would have had to spend endless hours in the library developing a technique which they can now work on in their normal homework time within their own homes, using such excellent paperback references as Jeans' *Growth of the Physical Sciences* (Premier, 50 cents and easily the best buy in the field), Van Melsen's *From Atomos to Atom* (Torchbooks, $1.45),

Dreyer's *History of Astronomy, Thales to Kepler* (Dover, $2.00), and the two volume set on the *History of Science and Technology* (Penguin, $5.00 a set). All are excellent survey books in their field.

6. Paperbacks can do all of the preceding at far less expense than would be incurred with hardcover books. It is obvious that the demands created by the FOS course were enormous. No single hardcover book could possibly meet all the requirements of such a course. The choice was simple: adjust the course outline to coincide more closely with the available books or rely entirely on the use of paperback books for the reference materials needed in the course. It has been very satisfying to discover that the stringent demands of the FOS curriculum have been met with reasonable expense through the use of paperback books. A single example would suffice: An outstanding reference on the history of science is the Addison-Wesley edition of the *Foundations of Modern Physical Science.* However, for the price of just two of these hard-cover editions, we have been able to supply every student in the course with his own copy of Jeans' *Growth of the Physical Sciences.* A good investment? I should say so!

PAPERBACKS SCORE!

It is still too early in the year to assess completely the results of the pilot course in "Foundations of Science." At first, there was considerable consternation among students about the lack of a single book to lean on. There was a desire among students for specific assignments of specific pages in a specific book. To be sure, there is still frustration among students; this frustration is now, however, the normal frustration any researcher feels when, on occasion, he has difficulty in locating information; it is not the frustration arising from not knowing *how* to look. That is, the hypothesis that a paperback library is a useful tool in developing research techniques appears, at the moment, to be well founded.

One other advantage of such a library is becoming apparent. It seems that this method of learning serves also as a motivational technique. The evidence for this is in the wide array of questions raised by students resulting more from their own reading than from any direct assignments. Further, the tendency of students to mention paperbacks which they have discovered on their own indicates a broadening appreciation of the materials available to them in carrying on research.

In general, it seems safe to say that much of the credit for any successes achieved in FOS must be given to the use of paperback books. Such books have released both students and teachers from the mental lock-step of a single standard textbook and allowed them to become free to learn and to teach the appropriate and desirable and not just what "the book" directs.

Paperbacks for Bright Students [3]

Helen Maestri, Librarian, Benjamin Franklin Senior High School, New Orleans, Louisiana

There is in our library a shelf reserved only for paperbacks; from it a student may take and keep any book he wants, provided he replaces it with one of his own. If, after he has read the paperback, he wishes to exchange it for another title, he is free to do so. In other words, a single paperback, 25 cents or $2.00, new or used, but in good condition, entitles a student to use the shelf for his three years at Franklin. All replacements, of course, must be approved by the librarian or one of the instructors.

"Why such an arrangement?" is a question often asked by the many visitors who come to our library. An answer requires a description of our school.

Benjamin Franklin Senior High School, which is now in the third year of its existence, is a public school for intellectually superior students only. To be admitted, boys and girls must have an IQ of at least 120 and, to remain, must maintain a general average of 85. They not only carry a heavy schedule of five academic courses instead of the usual four, but also go at an accelerated pace. These high standards, rather than discouraging the students, whet their appetite for more information and arouse their interest in more and more fields of knowledge.

Consequently, after the library has met the demands of our enriched curriculum, there is very little money left to purchase books in hard covers that would satisfy all the varied recreational needs of our mentally alert students. So our shelf of paperbacks came into existence in the spring of 1958 with four of my personal paperbacks, namely, *Six Great Modern Short Novels*, Lawrence's *Sons and Lovers*, Orwell's *1984*, and a 1955 edition of *Good Read-*

[3] Source: *Junior Libraries*, January 1960. Copyright © 1960 by R. R. Bowker, Co.

ing prepared by the Committee on College Reading of the National Council of Teachers of English.

It certainly did not seem a propitious beginning, but it proved otherwise. At first the only students who patronized the shelf of paperbacks were boys who used it to exchange their science fiction. As time passed, however, not only did students with interests other than science fiction use it, but also some of our faculty members contributed a few of their paperbacks. Today—at the present moment of writing—we have on the shelf a diversity of subjects with titles in the humanities predominating, as the complete list, given below, will show.

Psychology: *Successful Living,* Chesser.

Hobbies: *The Postage Stamp,* Williams.

Social Studies: *The Far East,* Bain; *The Romans,* Barrow; *The U.S. Political System,* Coyle; *One's Company,* Fleming; *Green Hills of Africa,* Hemingway; *American Diplomacy, 1900–1950,* Kennan; *The Way of Life,* Lao Tzu; *The Voice of Asia,* Michener; *The History of the World,* Sedillot; *Spotlight on Asia,* Wint.

Fine Arts: *Ballet,* Amberg; *A Popular History of Music,* Harman; *Ballet,* Haskell.

Autobiographies: *A Life of One's Own,* Field; *The Seven Storey Mountain,* Merton.

Literature: *In Search of Theatre,* Bentley; *Discovery* (1954); *A Short History of English Drama,* Evans; *The Idea of a Theater,* Ferguson; *New Poems by American Poets,* Humphries, editor; *American Essays,* Shaw, editor; *A Book of English Essays,* Williams, editor.

Fiction: *Peonies and Ponies,* Acton; *Veronica's Veil,* Cooper; *A Tale of Two Cities,* Dickens; *House of Seven Gables,* Hawthorne; *The Steep Ascent,* Lindbergh; *Of Human Bondage,* Maugham; *Come Away, Death,* Mitchell; *Mid-Century, an Anthology of Distinguished Contemporary American Short Stories.*

The phrase "at the present moment of writing" was used advisedly, because our shelf of paperbacks is an ever changing one. Note that there are not any science fiction titles presently available. Gone also are my original four contributions. The boy who selected *Six Great Modern Short Novels* told me he was keeping it for his personal library, as he wanted to reread Katherine Anne Porter's *Noon Wine* and William Faulkner's *The Bear.* The former was "superb" and the latter was "wild." *Good Reading* was also selected as an addition to a personal library. The girl who took it said it was well named, because it was the best reading list she had ever found. Needless to say, these remarks made me happy, as I had hoped the shelf of paperbacks would serve another valuable purpose—that of stimulating the student to acquire a library of his own.

Mathematical paperbacks, as far as most of our boys are concerned, are an excellent incentive for the purchasing of books. None of them have ever been placed on the shelf by our students—who cherish them too much to part with them. A few titles which have been in our paperback collection for very brief periods have been contributed by faculty members and friends of the school. Such titles as Gamow's *One Two Three . . . Infinity* and Mott-Smith's *Mathematical Puzzles* arouse in our boys a desire to read as well as to own. So some of them have purchased these titles or others of a similar nature at our local bookstores.

Use of Paperbacks With Slow Students

More Reading Means Fewer Drop-outs [1]

Helen McDonnell, Teacher, Wall High School, Belmar, New Jersey

With increasing emphasis being placed on reducing the number of high school drop-outs, the problem of the "slow" or "reluctant" reader must receive more attention. Yet we may find difficulty in comprehending the problems of the slow reader, for rarely does the teacher's background contain anything remotely resembling the combination of low achievement and intellectual frustration that have been his lot since his early years. The closest analogy I can find is the difficulty I once had in reading a German novel after only two years of college German. I discovered that I had to look up practically every fourth word, became discouraged, and put the book aside. If I had been better at German, or if the novel had been more interesting, I might have finished it. My situation was like the slow reader's, but with one difference. Reading materials that *will* interest the slow reader are always available.

Let me describe an experience I had with a group of 17 "reluctant" 10th graders. According to the *Gates Reading Survey,* in October their reading ages ranged from 9.1 to 15.2 with a median of 12.10. This was the first such group I'd taught, and I wanted to succeed; but my first efforts failed. I could break only briefly through the outer layer of suspicion and intellectual apathy before it closed in again, leaving me discouraged. Finally, realizing the heart of the problem was in reading difficulty, I embarked on an experiment. I have always been an avid reader because I enjoy books. Enjoyable books, then, would be my opening wedge. Teen Age Book Club books accumulated during the preceding year were supplemented with back copies of *Coronet, Reader's Digest,* and easy-to-read adaptations of classics in paperback; and these I took to school in my "book box"—a carton. I spread them on my desk and invited my slow readers to choose. Their apathy vanished as

[1] Source: Teen Age Book Club's *Memo: To Teachers,* © 1962 by Scholastic Magazines, Inc.

they crowded about, attracted by the bright covers. Before long they settled down at their desks, while I explained that Mondays were to be free reading days. Each student could read a book of his own choice until the last five minutes of the period, then note on a "comment sheet" his name, the book title, the pages read, and a short book comment. If a student wished to continue the book, he reserved it by signing on the inside cover. The comment sheets I collected weekly, returning them to be used again and so provide me with a continuous record.

At first I refused to allow books to be borrowed overnight. I wanted my students to look forward to their books, and I succeeded. My slow readers soon became my best TAB customers; they not only read my books, but bought and traded their own. And they had developed an interest in library books!

The results? My students learned to enjoy reading, to express themselves well (though not always grammatically) both orally and in writing; and they developed a gratifying critical ability. They learned to respect my judgment about books and other things as well; and I learned this important lesson: *books can be used to bridge the gap of suspicion and past failure that so often alienates slow students from their teachers.*

When I retested my class in May, all but three had improved. The median reading age had risen from 12.10 to 13.07. Greatest gainer was my best student, who attained a reading age of 17.04. Forging ahead of his chronological age of 16 years and 4 months, he was no longer a retarded reader. Second largest gainer was my slowest student, who tested at 10.11, a gain of 1 year and 10 months since October.

Was the low drop-out rate in this class a matter of coincidence? National statistics show that one out of three students leave high school before graduation. But, of the seventeen students who participated in my program from beginning to end, only two became drop-outs. One left the following year for personal reasons, and my oldest student, a boy nearing 18, failed because he had assumed no responsibility for homework, study, or class participation.

I believe that, if poor reading and its concomitant difficulties cause drop-outs, a major point of attack lies in learning how to encourage students to read. Easy books keyed to their interest are major weapons. The combination of book box and free reading period which proved effective in my class—not only as a reading stimulant, but as a meeting ground for teacher and student—may prove effective in your class too.

I Read to My Reluctant Readers [2]

Sister M. Antonia, O.S.F., St. Casimir School, Hammond, Indiana

At the beginning of the last school year, I was asked to teach two classes in developmental reading. Class 1 included the entire freshman class, and class 2, twenty sophomores and seniors who were doing failing or poor work as a result of poor reading.

The only materials at hand were the SRA Reading Lab, a few notes of experiments from other classes which had done some work in this area, and several brochures from Scholastic Book Services. I felt like the child who does not know how to swim, suddenly pushed into the "old swimming hole"!

From the very outset, I was determined that these classes were in no way going to be remedial reading classes. I had seen and experienced a complete balking at reading because of words and phrases which teen-age students felt belonged down in the primary grades. I wanted my students to read because *they wanted to.*

I introduced materials and aroused interest in both classes for Teen Age and Campus Book Clubs. Because the program was something new, everyone wanted to join. But after the novelty of the first books wore off, the students in the second class became a problem; the books were too long, the print was too small, and many similar excuses.

Then I recalled how much I enjoyed being read to in childhood and decided it would be worth the try with these young maturing adults (fifteen of the twenty students in class 2 were boys).

I asked that at least twelve of them purchase copies of *Ben Hur*— a Teen Age offering of that month. When the books arrived, instead of assigning the title, I told the students we would enjoy the book together. I would do the reading: they were to listen and follow. After a few periods of this, one of the very poorest students in the group asked if he might take *Ben Hur* to study hall, to read more of the story. It is at this point that the teacher feels rewarded for all her efforts!

After *Ben Hur,* this class then began *The Black Arrow,* which, left to themselves, they would have ignored. Once again it took several periods to gain the interest of the class. But before the half-way mark was reached I was able to begin a chapter and then have the class eager to read for themselves. April and May were spent in

[2] Source: The Teen Age Book Club's *Memo: To Teachers,* January 1964. Reprinted by permission of the author.

individual reading, principally of books recommended by the students to each other. Some of the favorites of this problem group were *Journey for Jennifer, To Tell Your Love, Hot Rod, One Night of Terror, Up Periscope,* and the Poe and Sherlock Holmes story collections.

Evidence that it was worthwhile came in reports from the history teacher as to what I had done to interest Jake, Richard, and Elmer in contributing to class discussions on current reading and affairs. (These boys had been the silent members of their classes during discussions.) Mary's mother made it a point to express her thanks to me at the close of the term. Mary, a sophomore, was reading on the fourth-grade level last September. She will never accomplish much in the line of academic achievement, but she will be able to hold her own on the social level of current and civic affairs.

My freshman students in class 1 were all able to maintain an average academic grade. As the year progressed, I introduced them in a very casual way to finding research information in the library through the use of the Periodical Index. They were thrilled to use so "grown up" a method of finding articles of interest. An entire six weeks was spent in doing research on a topic of their own choosing, in the library. Nine of the girls chose some phase of the nursing profession for their topics—an interest aroused by the *Sue Barton* books. Another decided on a paper about the UN after reading *The Highest Dream.* Several of the boys wrote on some phase of basketball or baseball with the aid of books from the Club.

Much of the work done by these ninth-graders would not pass on an upper level, but they did develop a working ability in doing research and writing a bibliography.

I feel that this Developmental Reading Program has brought great results in my classes.

The Battle of the Book: Slow Learners [3]

*David Zamchick, Social Studies Department,
Great Neck Senior High School, Great Neck, New York*

Do slow learners need to be spoon-fed through watered-down texts? Do they refuse to read when they share the responsibility

[3] Source: *The Clearing House,* September 1958. Reprinted by permission of the publisher.

of choosing their own selections? Are they incapable of reading mature books and arriving at mature meanings?

It would seem not! The reading problem of the so-called slow learner basically may be no different from that of the more able learner. This conclusion is borne out by four years of experimentation with paperbacks for slow learners in a high-school reading program. During this period so-called slow learners bought and read several thousand books. But quantity alone is hardly sufficient. What was the quality of the reading experience? *Hiroshima, The Bridges of Toko-ri, The Raft, Cress Delahanty, Magnificent Obsession,* and *A Night to Remember* were some of the most popular choices. Do these titles reflect a lack of concern with maturity? Are they significantly different from choices which might be expected from the more able reader? Again, it would seem not. The point is to get the so-called slow learner to read books of higher caliber with consistency.

How can a reading program enable him to do this? By providing class time in which to read, by careful planning of book discussions, and by questions designed to get underneath the characters' statements and actions. How characters act toward people, how people feel toward them, and what finally happens to them are questions which have made the more mature books come alive to many students. Even more specifically, through careful questioning a reader can be guided to material in his reading which has significance for him.

In discussing *Hiroshima,* Richard, an eleventh-grade pupil whose parents were separated, doubted that people who survived the bombing could ever make their lives whole again. Part of his conversation with his teacher follows:

These people have little to live for. Families are gone, friends are missing, nothing is the way it was before. Yet many continue to live! How do some of these people face their despair? Dr. Sasaki, for example?

"He's the young doctor, isn't he? Well, he was kept so busy taking care of others he couldn't think of himself. Besides, that was his job, helping others. The only ones who couldn't really help were the very young people."

How do these young people react to the bombing?

"They weren't as scared after it was all over. They became sick from radiation but they weren't too scared."

Which of these young people interested you the most, Dick?

"I remember Mrs. Nakamura's boy, Toshio, the best. He had a cousin who was a kind of hero to him. He was killed during the bombing while he was working in a factory. Toshio keeps getting nightmares about this."

Perhaps Toshio was reminded of his father who was killed earlier during the war. At any rate, how does he feel about being alive?

"Well, it gets to be a kind of adventure with him. He doesn't mind talking about what happened. In fact, at the end of the book he writes an essay about what happened and how he felt about it. He felt worse about his friends' mothers who were wounded and killed."

Why does he feel this way?

"I don't know! Maybe it's because his own mother was near him and he could always depend on her. She gave him strength. Some of the other kids weren't so lucky. I remember a boy and girl who seemed to act happy but were always breaking down and crying for their mother who was thought lost or killed until they were finally returned to her."

That's interesting! Why do you suppose these people behaved so differently?

"I'm not sure. The only thing I can think of is that maybe it's better to have one parent around, as Toshio had, than none."

There may be five, ten, or more books readied for discussion. The purpose is to explore the picture of life, people, and ideas gained by student readers. There are few final answers but many questions which are designed to provoke thought beyond a given class session.

It is always essential, however, to prepare for reading groups and to anticipate the variety of problems brought by these groups to the classroom. The early days of the school term, therefore, are spent in talking about reading, making mental notes of possible reading interests, and getting destructive feelings out in the open.

What destructive feelings? Jim, an eleventh grader, considered a perennial troublemaker, makes it clear right at the start. "This is my third reading class. What can *you* do to help me?" "Don't know yet," is the reply. "Maybe to begin with we'll try to find out what you might like to read." Ed, in the same group, casual almost to the point of laziness, puts it differently: "I never read much. What makes you think I'm going to change all of a sudden?" "You're not likely to change in a hurry," he is told, "but you may be surprised at how much you will accomplish during the year."

Blunt feelings? Yes! They illustrate the chip on the shoulder of the boy who is just worried enough to think you might knock it off. Jim and Ed are in the awkward position of thinking they are losers no matter what the choice. Their texts are potent educational dice and they suspect they are loaded. When attention is focussed on only one or two texts, good as they may be, the injury done them is compounded. However sprightly the covers and colorful the illustrations, the textbook means unpleasantness and failure to these students, and the pill remains sour to them, in spite of the sweeteners.

Jim and Ed need to participate fully in the program. But participation which has vitality and meaning comes only from a broad reading foundation. Here the motivation of the slow learner has to be recognized. He has a narrow base of proven interest, yet a vast potential for future reading. The primary aim is to reach that narrow base. Fresh reading enthusiasms need to be developed and nurtured. This requires a classroom library spanning many desires and interests. A surfeit of plenty—not ten, twenty, or thirty volumes but a library of hundreds of bright, sparkling paperbacks inviting to eye and hand can and should enrich the reading classroom.

Sandy, who maintained a sullen silence during our initial discourse or muttered "I don't like to read," perks up almost immediately. "These aren't regular schoolbooks?" she inquires. She is told some are not, though others may be. Soon two or more books are clutched possessively to her. Readers at this point are ready to assume their responsibilities as well as to enjoy their library privileges. They are urged to use good sense in organizing the library efficiently. Sandy, whose school record indicates suspected thievery, is asked to be class librarian to remind people of their responsibilities and to collect fines. She is surprised but genuinely pleased to be considered for the post. She consents to serve and leaves with one book, the class rules permitting only one book at a time to a reader. She is now more than willing to wait her turn for the others.

But the classroom library is only one front in the battle for the book. Another skirmish is getting the so-called slow learner to take pride in owning books. This is a major break-through against reader resistance. A book in the home, close at hand, is worth a hundred anywhere else. This phase of planning was thoroughly investigated during earlier discussions. Many pupils then indicated owning a book was distasteful to them. Bill, an exuberant tenth grader, with a hooting laugh and some vigorous headshaking, crystallized the feeling of his group with "I never owned a book in my life."

How can this attitude be dealt with? It is vehement, often un-reasoning, and sometimes permeated with fear and resentment. Again, the ownership of a book has to be made tempting, no less tempting than the introduction of a library to spice reading interest. It may also bear the distinction of seeming to be apart from regular English work, for forbidden fruits apparently taste the sweeter. Once books are made palatable, it is wise to capitalize on a trait common to many teen-agers: They do not like to stand alone, to be too different from anyone else. This applies to reading as well. When three-quarters or more of a group are participating in library activities or engaged in selecting books for personal libraries, one does not like to be off on the side lines watching.

The same Bill, some time removed from his comment above, recently volunteered, "In the past three years I've bought forty books and do you know, I've read almost all of them." When asked if he could remember his earlier comment, he shrugged and said, "No one at home owned books. It seemed to be important so I tried it." When pressed if it were important to him now, he replied, "I've got my own library and I bought the books myself. I don't think I wasted the money."

What does such a program accomplish? Time and opportunity to select books have been arranged. Readers have the books in their hands. They read because they are interested. They are involved with material of their own choosing which has meaning to them. The proofs of their reading, thinking, and speaking have been ex-amined.

Through such treatment, so-called slow learners can be reached. And when they are reached and touched beyond their walls of re-sistance, they read more—hundreds of books more. Isn't this the crux of their problem? They are provoked to think more about their reading and are inclined to write more. Thus reading, in a vital sense, sparks the growth of the so-called slow learner. But it is not splintered beyond recognition. It is a unified whole from which comes his willingness to participate—to speak, listen, think, and write. And isn't this, after all, the aim of every reading teacher?

Library Use of Paperbacks

The Supermarket Come-On [1]

*Jane Manthorne, Readers Adviser for Young Adults,
Boston Public Library*

Eric Goldman, professor of history at Princeton, commented recently on the impact of paperback books: "Who can fail to be fascinated in horror or in bedazzlement or in some combination of the two, at the rows of little volumes? Book after book has its supermarket come-on. The paperback shelves are a seven-alarm fire of color and design tricks." [a]

This supermarket come-on was used by the Boston Public Library in a trial run with paperbacks among young adult readers of ten of our branch libraries. We started with questions such as "Will young people respond as they do to drug store displays?" "Will the paperbacks all go missing?" "Will they be in tatters after the first circulation?" "Will we reach nonreaders?" Now, one year after the experiment began, we have the answers—answers, incidentally, which have launched us full sail "on a sea of paperbacks."

A DECADE BACK: NO IMPACT AT ALL

In 1950, the supervisor of home reading services wrote a memo to the chief librarian, recommending the purchase of paperbacks "to make available in economic fashion the large number of popular titles on reading lists." In 1951 we refurbished the open shelf department, an attractively modern recreational reading center within the Central Library building. Paperbacks were included, intershelved with hardcovers.

The first experiment made no impact whatsoever, mainly for two reasons: title selection and format. Remember the paperback in 1951? The sterile imprisonment of Montaigne and Vergil and

[a] Eric Goldman. "Survival in a sea of soft covers." *N. Y. Times Book Review,* Paperback Books Section, 1963, p. 1.

[1] Source: *School Library Journal,* January 15, 1965. Copyright © 1965 by R. R. Bowker, Inc.

Rochefoucauld in bland, unadorned softcovers? This was the caliber of our offering—literary classics, Latin poets, essays, books
which do not create circulation cyclones in hardcover, let alone in
drab papercover. Thus our first attempt was doomed really by the
undeveloped, larval stage of paperbacks themselves. We were ready
for them, but the paperbacks were not ready for us.

PAPERBACKS 1964

Our 1964 experiment was directed to young adult readers for
recreational reading, with these goals: "to stimulate and motivate
readers and slow starters alike. . . . The paperback will supplement, not be a substitute for, the reading of books in the permanent
collection." Would paperbacks fill the ceaseless demands for science
fiction, mysteries, Dr. Tom Dooley, *Dear Abby,* and love stories?
Were they really as cheap as they seemed?

For our trial run we selected ten branch libraries representing
a variety of communities, readership, proportion of young adult
use, and strength of resources. To each branch went a free-stand-
ing, rotating wrought iron rack and a paperback collection of a
hundred titles. For the sake of speedy preparation and economy
the paperbacks were not reinforced in any way or cataloged. The
only preparation consisted of library and branch stamping, book
pocket, and book card marked with author, title, and "PB." The
accompanying list of titles served as a checklist, accession sheet,
and circulation record.

Librarians in the ten pilot branches were asked to watch public
reaction and use at every stage from arrival of books to discontinua-
tion. Although the books selected were geared to the tastes of
young people 14 to 18 years old, and the experiment supervised by
the specialist in service to teenagers, there were no barriers to
readers of other age groups.

"NOTHING HAS NOT GONE OUT"

Hours after the racks were placed on branch floors they were
cleaned bare. One branch called for help when the experiment was
only a few days old. Staff members, it seemed, were embarrassed
by the emptiness of the rack and were constantly moving the holder
in and out of the workroom in a now-it's-empty, now-it's-not
routine.

In her breathless appraisal of how her public was responding, one
usually articulate librarian volunteered excitedly that "nothing has

not gone out at all," and then trying to retrieve half of her double negative, added, "I mean to say, every book has circulated to someone." So popular were the paperbacks that an additional fifty titles were added in August; by last January ten new branch participants joined the experiment. In June paperbacks were moved into all branch libraries, and seventy-five new titles added. The venture was no longer an experiment, but, unequivocally, a success.

WHO WERE THE READERS?

The readers embraced all age groups from curious children to newspaper-reading octogenarians. Children accounted for 12 per cent of the first year's circulation, young adults for 57 per cent, and adults for 31 per cent. These figures we could determine easily. Beyond them, to the pressing query, "Were paperbacks reaching nonreaders?" we could offer answers based on careful observation rather than definite statistics. Asked to what degree better-than-average, average, or nonreaders were reached, librarians responded as follows:

	a great deal	sometimes	hardly ever
Better-than-average	4	2	2
Average	9	1	
Nonreaders	2	5	2

Many sample impressions were reported by branches, among them: "On the first day of circulating paperbacks two boys ambled in, spotted the rack of paperbacks, showed disbelief, then departed. A while later they were back with three buddies (and library cards) in tow."

"Those who read the better books in hardcover seem to be attracted to paperbacks while the Marjory Hall set (teen romance readers) and the sweet-old-lady group were not interested."

"Young adults are willing to read more mature books in paperback format that they would never begin in hardcover editions."

Other branches reported: "Nonreaders come in for an hour or two to read paperbacks *a great deal*."

"Our collection is used largely by students to supply titles on the high school reading list."

"An elderly patron who comes in each day just to read the papers spent a full morning with Adler's *Thinking Machines*."

"Two or three Cavanna-DuJardin-Emery readers have become

Stewart-Whitney-Holt readers by starting with paperback copies of the latter."

"One young adult complained that he never gets a chance to read the paperbacks he takes home because his father reads them—and his father is not a library patron!"

Over and over again our readers extolled paperbacks for their easy selection (gay covers), for their portability. Several teenagers found them handy at ball games ("read one while waiting my turn at bat") and beach outings. We believe this, since several water-damaged copies looked as if they had been wrapped in swimming trunks.

SIDELIGHTS ON CIRCULATION

Circulation figures did reveal branch patterns of paperback popularity. We totaled the hardcover circulations of our branch participants, found what percentage of the total belonged to each branch and then did the same with paperback circulations for the same period. We discovered that the ratio of paperback to hardcover reading rose quite consistently among our branches with less than a hundred thousand circulation. For example, a branch responsible for only 10 per cent of the hardcover circulation achieved 19 per cent of the paperback circulation. Our busiest branch which accounted for 25 per cent of the hardcover circulation among the participants realized only 17 per cent of the paperback total. We can't conclude *why* this is so, only that "it happened that way."

BOOK SELECTION: "PACKAGE" LIBRARIES

One hundred titles, all previously approved for young adult collections (in some cases under different titles or in different formats) made up package collections which were duplicated tenfold, one for each of ten branch libraries.

Because these packages were for recreational reading, classics were kept to a minimum. Exceptions were the Brontes' *Jane Eyre* and *Wuthering Heights* and two plays by Shakespeare. The selections offered a full reflection of favorite teenage subjects: Gothic romance in Holt's *Kirkland Revels* and DuMaurier's *Rebecca;* science fiction, humorous fiction, and essays such as books by Guareschi, Jean Kerr, Wibberley, and Abigail Van Buren; World War II history and personal narrative; teen romances; mystery stories; and "end-of-the-world" themes such as Frank's *Alas, Babylon* and Miller's *Canticle for Liebowitz.*

We tried to balance girls' and boys' tastes in literature, but of the one hundred titles only about thirty-five were truly favorites with girls. We also tried to follow the ratio of adult to young adult titles recommended by the American Library Association (80 per cent adult to 20 per cent young adult), and came up with 84 per cent adult to 16 per cent teen titles.

MOST POPULAR TITLES

Our circulation counts on specific titles brought to light some surprises. First of all, the most popular, busiest titles in hardcover were not among our high-circulation paperbacks: *The Diary of Anne Frank, Lord of the Flies, Profiles in Courage,* and the Dr. Tom Dooley books. This suggests that it was our "reading" public, borrowers who had already read the above titles in hardcover, who used the paperback collections. A second interesting observation was that we had six consistently missing titles for which we had almost no circulation count from branches. We assume that they were popular since they disappeared so rapidly. They were: Felsen's *Hot Rod,* Walden's *My Sister Mike,* Verne's *Mysterious Island,* Barnett's *The Universe and Dr. Einstein,* Van Buren's *Dear Teenager,* and Wibberley's *The Mouse that Roared.*

Top preferences among adults were for suspense and mystery fiction: MacLean's *Fear Is the Key,* Hubbard's *Sister Simon's* murder case, Holt's *Kirkland Revels,* and three "Gothics" by Mary Stewart.

Young adults and children joined together in putting Kerr's *Please Don't Eat the Daisies* and Cavanna's *Scarlet Sail* among their top choices. Shakespeare and science were consistently unpopular with young adults.

HOW LONG DID THEY LAST?

Gloomy Cassandras who forecast failure proved overwhelmingly wrong. Today, more than a year after the test started, here is the fate—far from alarming—of our first packages of one hundred paperbacks in eight [b] branches:

Still in circulation:	362 or	45%
Discontinued for reasons of wear, missing pages, etc.	169 or	21%
Presumed missing	244 or	31%
Overdue, lost and paid for, etc.	25 or	3%

[b] Because two branches were unable to maintain full statistics we have figures for eight branches—eight hundred paperbacks.

Of the 362 paperbacks still in circulation, some have achieved circulations ranging from fifteen upwards to twenty-two per volume and *are still circulating.*

Of the 169 titles discontinued for reasons of wear, the average circulation per copy was eight times. Librarians have always felt paperbacks were cheap, but now we see definitely that a hardcover would have to amass fifty to a hundred circulations to match the economical cost-per-circulation of paperbacks.

As we embarked on our experiment, we thought that 75-cent paperbacks might survive more circulations than 50- or 25-cent volumes. This isn't so. Of our record-breaking paperbacks with circulations of fifteen or more, twenty cost 50 cents or less each. In some cases our 25-cent paperbacks are averaging a cost of 3 cents per circulation; our 35-cent paperbacks, 4½ cents per circulation; and our 40-cent paperbacks from 3 to 5 cents per circulation.

WHY DID THEY WEAR OUT?

As paperbacks made their frenetic circulation trips in and out of the libraries, they were watched carefully for the first signs of wear and tear. (We did not wish to circulate soiled wares.) Then, prior to discontinuing, each worn-out or damaged or defaced paperback was routed to the Central Library for careful examination to determine condition and apparent cause for removal from circulation. We found that 28 per cent of our withdrawn copies were removed because covers were completely off although bodies of the books were completely intact; 33 per cent were removed because of loose pages throughout; and 12 per cent were removed because back covers were missing. Two groups of paperbacks, those with white covers, which quickly become soiled, and those with center inserts of illustrations, are destined for rapid ruination. The greater weight of illustration-inserts appears to strain adhesion to the backing, and the pictures fall out.

RESULT: A PAPERBACK POLICY

So successful was our paperback experiment with young adults that on May 6, 1964 the Boston Public Library announced a paperback policy for young adults *and* adults in *all* branch libraries. This policy divides the acquisition of paperbacks into two areas. Paperback originals or quality paperbacks, i.e., printings of "titles of substance," will be treated like hardcovers—passed through Book Selection Committee, included with hardcovers on purchase lists, given regular processing, regular charging; mass market titles —recreational, popular, high-interest items—will be handled with "less formality," in the manner of our experiment.

In conclusion we might quote Eric Goldman again in regard to his reluctant acceptance of paperbacks: "So, like the rest of us I suppose, I am hooked, irretrievably hooked, by the paperbacks."

The Private School: Paradise for the Paperback [2]

Richard Tyre, Chairman, English Department,
Germantown Friends School, Philadelphia, Pennsylvania

Our private paradise is a good fourth of a tennis-court-sized, senior English classroom where the "Browsers' Bookstore," run by the seven-man English department, lures the buyers: 350 students in seventh to twelfth grade, and they buy over a thousand paperbacks a year—voluntarily! This does not include any class texts. It sounds like a paperback bookseller's paradise and it is, but it is also a student's and teacher's paradise.

Germantown Friends School is a Quaker co-educational day school in Philadelphia extending from kindergarten to twelfth grade which prepares the majority of its students for college. Several years ago the history curriculum for ninth to twelfth grade was converted almost entirely to paperbacks and the English department has for many years been 85 per cent paperback.

So here is George Goodeye, the average Germantown Friends School upperschool student, who has been required to buy at least fourteen paperback books for his year's curriculum and then voluntarily buys at least another three from the Browsers' Bookstore, not counting all those that he buys outside school. Of course, we have our reading problems and reluctant readers as well as the Browsers' bugs who buy twenty or thirty titles a year, but I think some of the ground rules and subliminal merchandising techniques that the English department has developed in three years of making mistakes would help other private and public schools to interest more students in buying good reading material.

[2] Source: *School Paperback Journal,* December 1964. Reprinted by permission of the publisher.

We charge the students the full printed price and have used the profits so far to increase our stock and pay back the money that was advanced so that we could initially order books. The student has to pay with his own cash or personal I.O.U.—no charging to parents. This simplifies bookkeeping and it gives the student a more possessive attitude toward these books than the ones come by more easily. A book bought with lunch money or the carfare home has a lot more chance of being read intently.

Paperbacks over 95 cents just do not sell, no matter how flush the student or alluring the title, and the junior high school student will rarely go over 50 cents (except girls buying *Gone With The Wind*). Of our approximately 700 titles (about 200 in front-cover display racks and the rest, spine showing on book shelves), about 350 are modern fiction, biography, etc., 250 are the great classics, and 100 are special collections to cater to the outside reading of the history curriculum, the anthropology course, the seniors' work in current politics, and the social concerns of the Friends.

We answer the inevitable parents' complaints that certain books are too mature for a high school bookstore with the assurance that every book in the store is recommended by some teacher for some student. We believe strongly that an operation of this size can not be run entirely by students. Many books obviously will be inappropriate to our George Goodeye because of reading level or subject matter, so that a teacher is always hovering near. This is made easy because the store is located in the senior English classroom.

We have found several advantages for this to balance the disadvantages of inaccessibility when the classroom is used. The teacher in charge can be doing anything else and still "mind the store," the display racks are facing the doorway and forming a barrier that must be passed by each student to or from his desk. Most important of all, our English teachers can function during the class session as personal book advisors. I have found that the question: "What was the last book you really enjoyed?" can guide me almost unerringly to suggest the next purchase that will make the student not only relish the book but grow at the same time.

Incidentally, a single English teacher need not be tied down by this responsibility. We trade off during our free periods, before and after school, etc., and frequently we will switch rooms during class time so that all teachers can have the opportunity of using the room during a free reading period or during a book discussion in class. Let's face it, our goal is not just to sell books. It is, however indirectly we wish to handle it, to encourage the process of education, and for this some casual guidance helps.

If, however, two or three students are gathered in front of the rack, I tiptoe away: the best salesman is an enthusiastic fellow student who has read the book, and intense runs on a single title are characteristic of teen-age buying.

A few merchandising gimmicks do not demean our professional status as English teachers. We offer money-back guarantees; if the student takes a book home, starts it, and does not like it, he may bring it back for a full refund. Only about one student in a hundred ever does this.

Because the store is in a classroom, we frequently step to the racks in the middle of a class discussion and read a relevant passage from a book on display. (The title usually sells out five minutes after the class ends.) Think of the resources that the working teacher would have, 700 titles at his finger tips at all times! It almost makes up for the admitted added work of ordering, bookkeeping, and standing by while the store is open.

Here are a few *don'ts* we have discovered.

Don't associate the Browsers' Bookstore with the school's textbook store so that the air of freedom and adult reading is maintained.

Don't create the atmosphere that a student *has* to buy. We call it the "Browsers' " store to encourage the idea of just browsing, but, as retailers have discovered, this sells more books.

Don't place the displays where they cannot be supervised by someone responsible.

Don't close up right after school or early on Fridays or the day before vacation. Many students buy good books the way my wife buys hats—to indulge a happy anticipation or to celebrate the completion of a long grind. But even the unread book sitting on the shelf is a constant reminder to read.

Above all, *don't* regard the paperback book store as an auxiliary enterprise like refreshments at a football game. The books you are handling are the very bone marrow of the educated man. They can make the whole English curriculum seem worthwhile. But, more than justifying your emphasis on vocabulary, reading comprehension, and plot analysis, they can achieve for the student what the word "liberal" in "liberal education" has come to mean, a liberating of the mind from those rigid confines of the classroom, the locker room, the small community which the high school inevitably is, and from the teen-ager's own self-centeredness. These books introduce him to the broader truths and beauties which make up our civilization.

Book Fairs

Come to the Book Fair! [1]

Marjorie Au, Chairman of the Book Fair Committee,
Akron (Ohio) Council of the Parent-Teacher Association

"Come to the Book Fair!"

That is the annual invitation extended to children in Akron, Ohio public schools, thanks to the Akron Council of Parent-Teacher Associations. Their Book Fair project has been sponsored annually for the past six years as a service to the individual PTA units. The fair offers a selection of good books to children and their parents, and encourages and stimulates the lifelong habit of reading the best in literature.

In order to offer an approved and controlled list of books at the fair, a committee of parents, librarians, and teachers compiled a list suitable for elementary pupils, but ranging in reading levels from preschool through the high school level. This list is re-evaluated every two years with some titles dropped and new titles added. The present list contains 400 titles: 261 hardbacks, 50 Scholastic paperback books, and 100 other paperbacks.

The idea was to have a mobile fair—one that could travel from school to school, with sample books on display. Triangular racks with two ledges on each side, on which books could rest, were made. By placing the racks on tables, the books are displayed at the children's eye level. Floor racks with shelf areas are also used for displaying books.

At present, the entire fair consists of seven boxes of books, ten tables, ten table racks, and three floor racks. It can easily be moved from school to school by truck.

Each school, through its PTA, schedules the fair for one week. The fair materials are delivered to the school on a Friday. The school's Book Fair committee sets up the fair. Throughout the next

[1] Source: *Scholastic Teacher* (elementary edition), October 1965. Reprinted by permission from *Scholastic Teacher,* © 1965 by Scholastic Magazines, Inc.

week, classes "come to the fair" to browse and discuss the books with their teacher. On a "Wish List," each child notes certain titles that he would like to read or own. A complete book list with prices goes with each child. Thursday is usually designated as "sale day," when orders are taken on hardback books, and paperback books are sold directly over the counter. On Friday, the fair is packed up and moved on to another school.

Preplanning and publicity add much to the success of the Book Fair. The fair is enhanced with artwork and posters made by the children, with stories told by librarians, with plays enacted by the children, and with book characters portrayed by the children. All of these things build up anticipation.

The biggest problem used to be the delivery of an ordered book. To offset this difficulty, a room in a centrally located school was set aside to house an inventory of several hundred books sent on consignment. In this way, orders can be filled immediately from the inventory.

Although one purpose of the Book Fair is to sell books, another is to introduce children to good books, which can also be found in their neighborhood libraries. And these libraries always feel the after-effects of a fair through increased circulation.

That's evidence enough for the Akron Council of Parent-Teacher Associations to want to continue inviting Akron's children to "come to the Book Fair!"

THE FUTURE

A Look at the Future:
Hardcover Myth and Paperback Reality

SIDNEY FORMAN

*Professor of Education and Librarian,
Teachers College, Columbia University*

Librarians are bound by a complex of traditions which have served society and the library profession exceedingly well. The observance of and the practices which stem from these traditions have established librarianship as an honored profession charged with the care and administration of the world's stock of books. The librarians' responsibilities have been both custodial and distributive.

One basic custodial tradition—or perhaps assumption—which influenced the practice of librarianship is that the book is sacred. This tradition developed in the beginning of the Christian era when the writings of the church fathers were preserved on parchment, sewn together and flattened between boards. This treatment was, in fact, selected for the specific purpose of distinguishing these records from pagan writings, which were preserved on leather rolls. Furthermore, the influence of the Holy Bible, the only book familiar in the West for many generations, impressed on society the sacred character of the book which embodied the Word of God. The concept of the book being sacred was bolstered by the Hebrews and Moslems, whose religions are also book-centered.

A second set of traditions stems from the idea that each book is unique and irreplaceable. This was an obvious fact before the invention of printing, when books were laboriously

I wish to express my appreciation to Professor Ray Trautman, School of Library Service, Columbia University, for his helpful comments during the preparation of this article.

hand written in scriptoria. Even books produced on the early presses were notable for their individual differences. Published works had to be transported long distances to reach the widely separated individuals capable of buying and reading them. Most books were produced at great social cost and were, in fact, treasures which only the wealthy could afford. Institutions possessing book collections guarded them jealously. Their custodians established rigid rules governing their retention and restricting access to them. It is true that printing increased the availability and distribution of books, but the rules governing libraries were continued with little change. Furthermore, the market for books, handwritten or printed, was restricted by the limited literacy of the masses in a hierarchical, aristocratic society.

A third element basic to the custodial tradition of librarianship was the idea that the book was the record of man's thought and accomplishment. Libraries represented man's cultural heritage. It was accepted that the cultural record embodied in books—the flywheel of the social order—had to be passed on to succeeding generations if society was to enjoy any kind of continuity and stability.

The traditional custodial assumptions of librarianship are held up to question by the appearance of the modern, paperback book. This is not to say that in format paperbacks are new; they are as old as printing itself. *But there are distinguishing characteristics which make the modern paperback unique.*

The most important characteristics of the modern paperback are its designed impermanence and relatively low cost. The modern paperback may also be identified and defined as a book convenient in weight, size, and shape. For many readers it appears to represent a physical and psychological break with the past. The paperback's characteristics are further defined by the development of new channels of distribution and new techniques of production. The distribution apparatus includes the network of news and magazine wholesalers who supply tens of thousands of outlets. Production is based on the use of high speed rotary presses, improved adhesives, and low cost lacquered or plasticized cover stock. These factors, when considered together with an extension of democracy, the great population expansion bringing new masses into the stream of cultural and social life, and the expansion of productive capacity and material wealth, make of the paperback a new phenomenon, distinctively different from the book or the paperback of the past.

The modern paperback has shattered the tradition of the sacredness of books. The ground for this change was prepared by the secularization of society for which books were material objects to be used like all other objects. The basic concept was further eroded by the diversity of titles and subject content appearing in this new medium. About 35,500 titles are now recorded in *Paperbound Books in Print* (35,542 as of September 1965). The change was completed by the widespread distribution of paperback books possible only in an urbanized, democratic society with its high level of literacy. Almost a million paperback books are sold each day—more than 300,000,000 each year.

The paperback has also destroyed the concept that each book is unique: these books are produced in innumerable copies exactly alike. Recently developed machines produce and bind more than twenty thousand copies per hour. An edition may number in the hundreds of thousands.

The third concept of custodial librarianship, that the book is a segment of our cultural heritage which must be passed on to succeeding generations, is directly contradicted by the major characteristic of the modern paperback, its impermanence. The physical substance of the book, its paper, ink, adhesives, and cover will disintegrate in a relatively short time. Considerations of durability are not properly applicable to this kind of book. This combined with the inexpensive character of the paperback —one quarter of the publications retail at an average price of 65 cents—mark it as an expendable or consumable item. This is substantially true of even the more expensive quality paperback. This does not deny that the paperback is a significant element of our cultural heritage. Many books appear in paperback form only, and the critical notes which sometimes accompany reprints of classics are important aspects of twentieth century culture. These facts must not be ignored, particularly by the library profession which, in the last century, has so laboriously developed an extensive bibliographical apparatus. Librarians, however, particularly those in research institutions will have to find ways and means of preserving this segment of man's record, perhaps by special printings or by photographic processes.

The modern paperback then challenges the librarian's custodial traditions and practices. Neither sacred nor unique, the paperback represents an even greater challenge to the distributive functions of the librarian—his responsibilities in the realm of communications. For it is in fulfilling this role, of bringing to each individual the information he needs at the time and place that he needs it, that the librarian can be of the greatest service to mankind. Democratic and social institutions are dependent, as never before, upon a greater diffusion of knowledge and understanding. The concept of universal education, of providing free and equal opportunities for each individual to develop his potential is a prevailing reason for the design of American librarianship as well as education. The imperatives of our time suggest that librarians, in regard to their distributive functions, must diminish the gap between their theory and their practice. For this purpose the paperback is a basic tool.

A dramatic utilization of the paperback was the publication of the Armed Services Edition in World War II when the Government, between 1942 and 1946, purchased 1,324 titles in 123,500,000 copies at an average cost of 6.09 cents per volume and distributed them to millions who had never before done much reading. Another example is represented in the twenty-four dormitory-type libraries at the United States Military Academy made up of selected paperbacks which radically extended readership at a lower cost per unit than could be accomplished in the main library. For these collections, problems of administration and accountability were practically nonexistent. There are many other proposals and experiments which commend a wider utilization of paperbacks.

One is the suggestion by Professor Carl H. Melinot, of the Graduate School of Library Science, Syracuse University.

Professor Melinot urges that book collections for community college libraries be assembled using *Paperbound Books in Print* for selection and ordering as well as for a guide to holdings and location. While community colleges are the most rapidly growing sector of American education, the libraries are their most neglected area. Students in these institutions will continue to be short-changed until sufficient book stocks are made available in their libraries. Paperbacks may be used to meet the need speedily and economically. The idea may be equally applicable to many high school libraries.

In another instance, a successful experiment was carried out by the Fraser Valley Regional Library in British Columbia which initially purchased 15,300 mass-market paperbacks for an average cost of 32.7 cents each. After six months, 15 per cent of the total adult book stock accounted for 30 per cent of the circulation. Circulation alone, however, is not the *sine qua non* of library service. The librarian may do even better by referring the questioning reader to the availability and cost of paperback books for sale.

Much more needs to be done to make full use of this new type of book. To do so effectively the librarian must identify and analyze the impediments to improved service. He must then examine the particular characteristics of the paperback book, taking into consideration the available diversity of subject content as listed in *Paperbound Books in Print*. A solution is indicated whenever one or more of the characteristics of the paperback are relevant to the problem.

The unrealized potential of the paperback also challenges the publishing industry. For example, ways and means should be found to release in the United States the Ladder Series of books—the simplified editions of regular paperbacks now available overseas through the U. S. Information Agency at nominal prices of 10 or 15 cents. These are standard literary works, abridged to fit a 128-page format, and using limited vocabularies of one to five thousand words. There are a number of books for each vocabulary level. Such "easy readers" could help in any effort to reduce pockets of illiteracy in this country and enlarge the reading and buying public. The industry must solve the involved economic problems and extend the distribution of these books.

The paperback also calls to account the administrators of educational institutions who distribute, retrieve, and store worn textbooks because of their lasting qualities. How often is it more economical and more effective educationally to give youngsters single use texts that are up-to-date in content which they may retain to form the nucleus of a personal library?

In fact, the entire nation is challenged by the technology of the paperback. Benjamin Franklin's concern for education in 1731 impelled him to establish in Philadelphia a library ". . . to propagate Knowledge and improve the Minds of Men, by rendring useful Science more cheap and easy of Access. . . ." Far more than in Franklin's time, education today is recognized as the key to economic and social progress; and in most recent decades the concept of investment in education has become widely accepted. National political and social strength now require that information—that is access to man's cultural heritage—be as available as water at the town pump. To accomplish this purpose, the implication is intrusive that in several areas of library service it is more economical to give away paperbacks than to adhere to the traditional lending procedures. The very existence of the modern paperback calls into question many of the policies which govern libraries. Can a nation with a sufficiency of woodpulp, an advanced technology, and a high standard of living afford to administer its books as they were administered a hundred years ago? These considerations suggest that one worthwhile economical supplement to the structure of American education would be the establishment of paperback libraries within fifty miles of any point in the United States from which any person could draw any materials needed. This could be extended to make freely available any segment of the entire range of recorded human knowledge. When this is done, new lustre will be added to the traditions of librarianship, and the librarian will cross the threshold of the paperback revolution.

SELECTED BIBLIOGRAPHY

A Selected Bibliography of Periodical Articles, Pamphlets, and Books on Paperbacks in Education

HAROLD H. LASKEY
Paperback Exhibits Director,
The Combined Book Exhibit, Inc.

Alexander, Mark. A Novel Approach to Social Studies. *School Paperback Journal,* January 1965.

Aley, Howard C. Teaching the ABC's of Economics via the School Bookstore. *School Paperback Journal,* October 1965.

Allen, M. Paperbacks Go to School. *School and Community,* May 1962.

Allen, P. H. Current Children's Paperbacks. *School Library Journal,* May 15, 1965.

Anderson, Dorothy J. Good Reading for Youth: Fever Sweeps Four States. *Top of the News* (ALA), December 1963.

Anderson, Scarvia B. Between the Grimms and "The Group": Literature in American High Schools (pamphlet), Educational Testing Service, Princeton, N. J., 1964.

Anderson, Vivienne. The Teachers College Paperback Conference. *School Paperback Journal,* December 1965.

Anthology Mythology (Untraditionally Speaking). *School Paperback Journal,* March 1965.

Arbital, Samuel. Paperbacks and the Election. *Scholastic Teacher,* September 30, 1964.

Arbital, Samuel. Paperbacks and the 1964 Elections. *School Paperback Journal,* November 1964.

Archer, Marguerite P. Behind the Boom in Books. *Scholastic Teacher,* October 7, 1964.

Archer, Marguerite P. The Book Boom. *Scholastic Teacher,* October 7, 1964.

Around Books (Teachers College Paperback Conference). *Saturday Review,* November 20, 1965.

Baehr, Margaret. 100 Outstanding Paperbacks for Elementary School Children. *Catholic Education,* October 1965.

Barbe, Walter B. Individualized Reading. *Scholastic Teacher,* October 7, 1964.

Bass, J. A. Paperbacks for Distributive Education. *School Management,* August 1962.

Batton, Delma. Alice at the State Library. *Top of the News* (ALA), January 1965.

Beauchamp, Robert. Variations on a Theme. *Scholastic Teacher,* January 17, 1964.

Beauchamp, Robert. What's New in Paperbacks? *Scholastic Teacher,* January 17, 1964.

Beauchamp, Robert. Bridging the Gap. *School Paperback Journal,* November 1964.

Benedict, Stewart H. Paperbacks in an Experimental College Course. *Studies in the Mass Media* (NCTE), December 1963.

Benedict, Stewart H. Teach Philosophy in the Secondary School? *School Paperback Journal,* March 1965.

Bentley, Martha C. Children's Paperbacks: A Long Hard Look. *School Library Journal,* January 15, 1965.

Benyei, Paul, McLaughlin, Frank, and O'Donnell, Cornelius. 3 by Shaw. *School Paperback Journal,* December 1965.

Bernstein, Abraham. *Teaching English in High School* (New York: Random House, 1961).

Better Libraries for Today's Child. An *Instructor* Library Supplement, November 1962.

Billings, Jane K., and Paulson, Joan A. Honors Reading Program in Senior High School. *English Journal,* May 1965.

Bogart, Max. The New Jersey Report. *School Paperback Journal,* September 1965.

Bogart, Max. Paperback Book Study in New Jersey. *Scholastic Teacher,* October 28, 1965.

Bogart, Max, and Fink, Rychard. Paperbound Books in New Jersey Public Schools (pamphlet). New Jersey State Department of Education, Trenton, 1965.

Bolger, Philip, Schwietert, Louise, and Urell, Catherine. Comparison of Paperback and Hardcover Textbooks as to Price, Durability, and Educational Merit: Final Report on the Pilot Project (mimeographed report). Bureau of Educational Research, Board of Education of the City of New York, January 1964.

Bolger, Philip, Schwietert, Louise, and Urell, Catherine. The Paperback Studies: Summary Statement (mimeographed report). Bureau of Educational Research, Board of Education of the City of New York, April 1964.

Bolger, Philip, Schwietert, Louise, and Urell, Catherine. Study of Certain Factors Relevant to the Use of Mass Market Paperbacks in High School Literature Courses (mimeographed report). Bureau of Educational Research, Board of Education of the City of New York, April 1964.

Bonn, George S. Science Belongs in a Library. *Library Journal,* January 1, 1961.

Book Clubs Help Children. *West Side News and Morningsider* (Supplement), October 21, 1965.

Book Fair Bill o'Fare. *School Paperback Journal,* February 1965.

Book Fairs: A Symposium. *Scholastic Teacher,* April 29, 1965.

Bookmobile: Bookstore on Wheels Visits High Schools. *Scholastic Teacher,* April 29, 1965.

Bossone, Richard M., and Nicolet, Eric J. What Happened in Hemet, California? In *Classroom Practices in Teaching English* (Champaign, Ill. National Council of Teachers of English, 1965), pp. 59–62.

Bourgeois, Yvonne, and Lilley, Dorothy. Blueprint for Paperbacks in the High School Library. *School Library Journal* (Children's Section), January 15, 1963.

Boutwell, William D. Paperbacks: The Best Invention Since the Sandwich. *NEA Journal,* October 1959.

Boutwell, William D. The Paperback Boom. *Studies in the Mass Media* (NCTE), December 1961.

Boutwell, William D. *Using Mass Media in the Schools* (New York: Appleton-Century-Crofts, 1962).

Boutwell, William D. Two New Trends: Paperbacks, Book Clubs. *The Instructor,* November 1962.

Boutwell, William D. The Children's Crusade for Reading. In Butman et al., *Paperbacks in the Schools* (New York: Bantam Books, 1963), pp. 50–61.

Boutwell, William D. i/t/a Paperback Series. *Scholastic Teacher,* March 4, 1965.

Boyd, Marvin. How One Junior High PB Plan Works. *Scholastic Teacher,* March 13, 1963.

Brahm, W. Great Misconceptions? Every New Scientific Invention Death Knell of Reading and Libraries. *Library Journal,* February 1, 1965.

Brooks, Charlotte. School Library or Booketheque? *School Library Journal,* April 15, 1965.

Brooks, John. Look at the Paperbacks. *Consumer Reports,* June 1963. Excerpts: *School Library Journal,* January 15, 1964.

Brooks, John. Scanning the Paperback Scene. *School Library Journal* (Children's Section), January 15, 1964.

Brother Clement David. The Paperback: A Trojan Horse? *The Catholic Educator,* January 1962.

Brown, F. W. Reading Unlimited. *Texas Outlook,* July 1962.

Brown, Ralph A. The Use of Paperbacks in High School Social Studies Classes. *School Libraries,* May 1962.

Bruell, E. Paperback Comes to Bremer High. *English Journal,* January 1962.

Bruni, Thomas G. Foreign Language Paperbacks. *Scholastic Teacher,* January 17, 1964.

Buelow, G. J. Paperback Miracle: An Inexpensive Library for Music Teachers and Students. *American Music Teacher,* January 1964.

Bureau of Independent Publishers and Distributors. The Paperback Goes to School, 1965–66 (pamphlet). Author, New York, 1965.

Burleson, Derek L. Operating a Classroom Book Club—Is It Worth the Time? *Curriculum News and Views,* May 25, 1961.

Burrows, David J. Paperbacks in College American Literature Courses. *Studies in the Mass Media* (NCTE), December 1963.

Butman, Alexander. Our Commitment is Major and Long Range. *School Paperback Journal,* October 1964.

Butman, Alexander. What's Social about Social Studies? *School Paperback Journal,* April 1965.

Butman, Alexander, Reis, Donald, and Sohn, David (Eds.) *Paperbacks in the Schools* (New York: Bantam Books, 1963).

Cambridge Logic Falling Down (Untraditionally Speaking). *School Paperback Journal,* May 1965.

Carline, Donald E. Elementary School Children Build Paperback Libraries. *Studies in the Mass Media* (NCTE), November 1961.

Carline, Donald E. Paperbacks in a College Reading Center. *Studies in the Mass Media* (NCTE), January 1963.

Carline, Donald E. Meeting in that Mysterious World. *Studies in the Mass Media* (NCTE), December 1963.

Carline, Donald E. Paperbacks for Curriculum Enrichment. *Scholastic Teacher,* March 4, 1964.

Carlsen, G. Robert. English for the Ungifted. *English Journal,* May 1961.

Carlsen, G. Robert. For Everything There Is a Season. *Top of the News* (ALA), January 1965.

Case for Bookburning: Political Pamphlets. *Christian Century,* November 11, 1964.

Cass, James. Books in the Schools (pamphlet). American Book Publishers Council, New York, 1962.

Catholic High School Library Survey. *Newsletter* (Catholic Library Association High School Libraries Section, Haverford, Pa.), Winter, 1964.

Chapin, J. R. Paperbacks on the Middle East for High School Use. *Social Studies,* February 1962.

Children Learn by Doing, Is Educator's Message. *West Side News and Morningsider* (Supplement), October 21, 1965.

Christian, L. Paperback Books Help School Libraries. *Ohio School Journal,* April 1964.

Cirker, Howard. Scientific Paperback Revolution. *Science,* May 10, 1963; Discussion: August 9, October 11, December 27, 1963.

Clancy, T. Hall of Defamers: Paperbacks a Major Weapon in Political Warfare. *America,* October 31, 1964.

Clark, Leonard H. Why Don't They Like History? *School Paperback Journal,* May 1965.

Clark, Leonard H. Social Studies and The Bridge over the River Kwai. *School Paperback Journal,* October 1965.

Clark, William A. The Humanities Program in the High School. *English Journal,* October 1962.

Clear, V. Paperback Pedagogy. *Saturday Review,* February 15, 1964.

Cleary, Francis X. Why Johnnie is Reading. *Education,* January 1962.

Cleary, Francis X. 100 Outstanding Paperback Books. *The Catholic Educator,* January 1963.

Clement, S. L. Why Paperback Textbooks are Worth Considering. *The Nation's Schools,* July 1962.

Cohen, David. Plainview Welcomes Paperbacks: A High School Library's Experience. *School Library Journal,* January 15, 1965.

Cohen, S. Alan. Using Paperbacks in the Secondary School. *Journal of Education,* April 1964.

Cohen, S. Alan. Have You Tried These Paperback Technics? *The Nation's Schools,* August 1965.

Combined Book Exhibit: A Peaceful Expansion. *Publishers' Weekly,* January 4, 1965.

Conference in October on Paperbacks in Education. *Publishers' Weekly,* March 8, 1965.

Cook, Joan. A Little Shop Sells Books to Children; Store in School Offers Quality Paperbacks to Youngsters. *New York Times,* November 18, 1963.

Corinth, Kay. The Teen-Age Girl and the Book Market. *Publishers' Weekly,* August 17, 1964.

Craig, Anne, and Rowell, John. What Books for the Young Adult? *School Library Journal,* October 15, 1964.

Crawford, Frank A. Paperback Book Fairs at Benjamin Franklin Junior High School. *Studies in the Mass Media* (NCTE), December 1963.

Crosthwait, C. Censorship and the School Library. *Wilson Library Bulletin,* April 1965.

Culkin, Rev. John M., S.J. Movies, TV, and Paperbacks. *Scholastic Teacher,* January 17, 1964.

Davis, O. L. Textbooks and Other Printed Materials: Paperback Books. *Review of Educational Research,* April 1962.

Deason, Hilary J. The Paperback in High School Science Instruction. *Science News Release* (AAAS), February 1962.

Deason, Hilary J. Reading and Thinking; The Road to Scientific Literacy. In Butman et al., *Paperbacks in the Schools* (New York: Bantam Books, 1963), pp. 98–111.

Deason, Hilary J. Paperbacks in an Age of Science. *Scholastic Teacher,* January 17, 1964.

Democracy in Education a Must, Whittier Asserts. *West Side News and Morningsider* (Supplement), October 21, 1965.

Deprived School Children Get Something To Keep. *West Side News and Morningsider* (Supplement), October 21, 1965.

DeYoung, Charles. Reinforcing Paperback Books. *School Library Journal,* January 15, 1960.

Donelson, K. L. Using Paperbacks: Some Why's and How's. *English Journal,* March 1964.

Dorros, Sidney. Paperbacks and Professional Growth. *School Paperback Journal,* December 1965.

Do Your Schools Have Paperback Bookstores? *School Management,* November 1960.

Dunford, T. A., and Grodhaus, D. W. Paperbacks at Parma. *Ohio Schools,* April 1961.

Durability Isn't Everything: Paperback Study Group Reports. *Publishers' Weekly,* October 5, 1964.

Ellsworth, R. E., and Wagener, H. D. *The School Library: Facilities for Independent Study* (New York: Educational Facilities Laboratories, 1963).

Elmes, Norman, Jr. Love's Labor Lost (It Seems). *Studies in the Mass Media* (NCTE), January 1963.

Elmes, Norman, Jr. Originals, Anyone? *School Paperback Journal,* September 1965.

Embree, Ainslie T., et al. A Guide to Paperbacks on Asia: Selected and Annotated (pamphlet). The Asia Society, New York, 1964.

Emerson, John B. Paperbound Books in the Independent School. In *Paperbound Book Guide for High Schools* (New York: R. R. Bowker, 1964).

Esbjornson, Ruth. On Being a Reader. *The Lutheran,* August 26, 1964.

Escarpit, R. Revolution in Books: Symposium. *UNESCO Courier,* September 1965.

Exploration of Creativity Urged as Schools' Goal. *West Side News and Morningsider* (Supplement), October 21, 1965.

Falke, M. H. High School Students Like Paperbacks. *Wilson Library Bulletin,* November 1960.

Fifty New Jersey Schools Engaged in Trade Paperback Book Study. *Newsletter,* New Jersey State Department of Education, January 1964.

Finch, Hardy R. How To Buy Them When You Need Them. *Scholastic Teacher,* January 17, 1964.

Finch, Hardy R. Juvenile Paperback Roundup. *Scholastic Teacher,* October 28, 1965.

Finch, Hardy R. Paperbacks for Teenage Readers. *Senior Scholastic* October 28, 1965.

Find Paperback Books Stimulate Slow Learners. *West Side News and Morningsider* (Supplement), October 21, 1965.

Fisli, Ruth. How Our Library Runs A School-Wide Book Club. *Scholastic Teacher,* March 13, 1963.

Fjelde, Rolf. Translation and the Repertory Stage. *Paperbound Books in Print,* February 1965.

Flaherty, D. L. Paperbacks in School. *America,* October 31, 1964.

Flayderman, Phillip C. A Frank Query: Paperbacks vs Hardcovers. *The Clearing House,* March 1965.

For a Child's Library: A Paperback Book List (Prepared for the Mohawk Valley Library Association by the children's libraries of Schenectady County Public Library). *School Library Journal,* January 15, 1965.

Forman, Sidney. Hardbound Myth and Paperback Reality. *School Paperback Journal,* October 1965.

Foster, Joanna. Exhibit Highlights at the Teachers College Paperback Conference. *Scholastic Teacher,* October 28, 1965.

Fox, Austin McC. New Kid in School; The "Buffalo Program" Makes Good: A Report on the Western New York High School Paperback Book Project (pamphlet). The Nichols School, Buffalo, N. Y.

Fox, Austin McC. The Buffalo Paperback Project: More than a Paper Moon. *Studies in the Mass Media* (NCTE), November 1961.

Francis, J. F. Preferences and Readability of Paperback Books. *Journal of Education,* April 1964.

Franklin, R. D. Game of Chicken: Some Librarians Afraid To Apply Standards, Pressured by Cries of Freedom. *School Library Journal,* October 15, 1964.

Free Paperbacks. *Scholastic Teacher,* December 2, 1964.

Freeman, Sara. Real Readin' Without the Reader. *Scholastic Teacher,* October 28, 1965.

French, W. First Year of the Paperback Revolution. *College English,* January 1964.

Gall, Morris. Paperback Gleanings: A Library for the Academically Talented. *Social Education,* November 1959.

Gall, Morris. Science Paperbacks in Social Studies. *Social Education,* December 1960.

Gall, Morris. Using Paperback Classics in the Social Studies. *Social Education,* March 1963.

Gall, Morris. The Teachers' Paperback Library. *Civic Leader,* May 6, 1963.

Gall, Morris. Paperbacks in the Social Studies. In Butman et al., *Paperbacks in the Schools* (New York: Bantam Books, 1963), pp. 82–97.

Gall, Morris. American History: A Hardcore of Soft Covers. *School Paperback Journal,* October 1964.

Gall, Morris. Professional Paperback Review. *School Paperback Journal,* March 1965.

Gall, Morris. The Junior Lines. *School Paperback Journal,* November 1965.

Gardiner, Harold C. Paperback Hurricane. *America,* November 4, 1961.

Garvey, William P. Wonder Weapon of Social Sciences. *The Catholic Educator,* September 1963.

Gemme, Francis R. The Scarlet Letter Coloring Book. *School Paperback Journal,* October 1965.

Gerhard, George. Some Notes on Paperbacks. *Studies in the Mass Media* (NCTE), December 1963.

Gerould, C. More Solid Reading between Soft Covers. *Natural History,* October 1961.

Gilbert, Christine B. The Influence of the Paperback. *School Libraries,* January 1963.

Gipe, M. W. Hardbound versus Paperbound Books: A Description of the California Study. *California Education,* June 1964.

Good Reading Program sponsored by U.S. Jaycees and A.L.A. Young Adult Services Division. Bulletins and booklists from John D. Burris, Jaycees Program Chairman, 1300 Greenhill Avenue, Holly Oak Terrace, Wilmington, Delaware 19809 or William J. Worrell, Pilgrim Book Society, 82 Pembroke Road, Akron, Ohio 44313.

Gordon, Edward. The Teacher and the Censor. In Butman et al., *Paperbacks in the Schools* (New York: Bantam Books, 1963), pp. 62–72.

Gordon, Galvy. Paperback Pilot Project. *School Library Journal,* January 15, 1964.

Grannis, C. B. Is This Edition Really Necessary? *Publishers' Weekly,* November 1, 1965.

Greenberg, Benjamin B. Studies Being Conducted of Paperback Revolution. *The Gist* of the Atlantic City Meeting (AASA), Third issue, 1964.

Grodhaus, David W. Paperbacks in the High School. *Ohio Library Association Bulletin,* April 1963.

Grogan, A. C. Paperback Books Invade the School Library. *Chicago Schools Journal,* February 1962.

Gross, S., and Steckler, P. B. (Eds.) *How to Run a Paperback Bookshop: A Basic Manual of Practical Information* (New York: R. R. Bowker, 1963).

Grunwald, Beverly. Searching Out the Paperbacks. *New York Times Book Review,* November 7, 1965.

Guzie, T. W. Paperbacks: A New Trend in High School Literature. *Catholic School Journal,* November 1960.

Hamlin, Arthur T. Development of the Student's Own Library. *The Educational Paperback Researcher,* Vol. 1, Jacksonville, Ill.

Handlin, Oscar. Libraries and Learning. *Atlantic Monthly,* April 1964.

Hannigan, J. A. Use of Paperbacks in High School Teaching. New York Society for the Experimental Study of Education Yearbook 1963.

Harmon, M. R., Jr. Selling Paperbacks . . . in the Classroom! *School Paperback Journal,* December 1964.

Hartz, F. R. Establishing a New Library with Paperback Books. *New York State Education,* April 1964.

Hartz, F. R. Paperback Books and the College Library. *Improving College and University Teaching,* Spring 1964.

Hawkins, Quail. Promoting, Planning and Producing Book Fairs. *Publishers' Weekly,* July 13, 1964.

Hechinger, Fred M. Revolution in the Classroom. *New York Times Book Review* (Paperback Book Section), January 10, 1955.

Hechinger, Fred M. Textbook Market Faces Revolution. *New York Times,* February 19, 1962.

Heiss, Warren. Reading and Mathematics. *School Paperback Journal,* February 1965.

Help for Slow Learners. *West Side News and Morningsider* (Supplement), October 21, 1965.

Hieber, Caroline E. Paperbacks for College-Bound Students. *School Library Journal,* January 15, 1964.

Higgins, V. Louise. The Soft Sell. *Studies in the Mass Media* (NCTE), March 1961.

High School Departments of English: Their Organization, Administration, and Supervision (Champaign, Ill.: National Council of Teachers of English, 1965). See especially: Organizing the Department, pp. 13–14; Curriculum, pp. 21–22; Organizing the English Department for Effective Instruction, pp. 44–46; The Role of the Department Chairman in Curriculum Development, pp. 48–53; and The Chairman's Role in Selecting Textbooks and Library Books, pp. 54–58.

Hillier, Richard L. The Bard in Paper. *School Library Journal,* January 15, 1964.

Hinchcliff, William E. A Modest Proposal. *Paperback Trade News,* September 1960.

Hinchcliff, William E. Potent Pellets: Two Proposals for Bold Use of Paperbacks in College, School and Public Libraries. *School Library Journal,* September 15, 1961.

Hinchcliff, William E. Potent Pellets: A Proposal for Bold Use of Paperbacks in Junior Colleges. *Junior College Journal,* March 1962.

Hinchcliff, William E. Ask the Young Man Who Owns One . . . Hundred. *Scholastic Teacher,* December 2, 1964.

Hinchcliff, William E. Abundant Good Books for an Affluent Society. *Improving College and University Teaching,* Summer 1965.

The Hip Pocket Library, in The Shape of Education for 1964 (pamphlet), by the editors of *Education U.S.A.,* 1964, pp. 15–17, National School Public Relations Association (NEA).

Hochwalt, Rev. F. G. Paperbacks: An Approach to Excellence, National Catholic High School Summer Reading Program. *Catholic School Journal,* September 1964.

Holtman, Eugene. Paperbacks and the Academic Library. *Ohio Library Association Bulletin,* April 1963.

Hoopes, N. Why a Book Fair? *Scholastic Teacher,* February 14, 1964.

Hoth, William E. The Paperback in the Teaching of English. In Butman et al., *Paperbacks in the Schools* (New York: Bantam Books, 1963), pp. 73–81.

Hoth, William E. Paperbacks and Professional Growth. *Scholastic Teacher,* October 28, 1965.

Houle, C. O. Two Revolutions and their Consequences. *ALA Bulletin,* July 1962.

How Libraries and Schools Can Resist Censorship (leaflet). American Library Association, Chicago, 1962.

How To Acquire Books under NDEA, etc. *Scholastic Teacher,* March 4, 1965.

How To Buy Books for Your School Library. *School Management,* May 1963.

How To Fortify Your Curriculum with Paperback Books. *School Management,* August 1963.

How To Make More Books Available to Your Students. *School Management,* November 1963.

How To Plan a Book Fair; Manual for A Successful Book Fair. *Scholastic Teacher,* February 14, 1964.

How To Start a School Paperback Bookstore. The Combined Paperback Exhibit in Schools (catalog). The Combined Book Exhibit, Briarcliff Manor, N.Y., 1964.

Humphrey, Hubert H. Paperback Attack on Poverty: Free Book Program for Needy Children. *School Library Journal,* May 15, 1964.

Humphrey Urges U.S. Book Blitz. *Scholastic Teacher,* March 4, 1965.

Hurley, Richard J. New Revolution on the Potomac. *Scholastic Teacher,* March 13, 1963.

Hurwitz, Howard L. New Paperbacks in the Social Sciences. *Scholastic Teacher,* December 2, 1964.

Hurwitz, Howard L. A Bonanza of American History Reprints (What's Happening in Social Studies?). *Scholastic Teacher,* February 11, 1965.

i/t/a Paperback Series. *Scholastic Teacher,* March 4, 1965.

James Baldwin Novel Attacked in Chicago. *Publishers' Weekly,* February 1, 1965.

Jarrett, James L. Great Books in Paperback. *Saturday Review,* March 23, 1963.

Jassey, William. The Modern Language Revolution Needs a Coordinated Paperback Program. *School Paperback Journal,* December 1965.

Jenkinson, E. B. Literature: In Sequence and in Earnest. *Secondary School English Notebook* (D. C. Heath), November 1962.

Jennings, Frank G. *This Is Reading* (New York: Teachers College Press, Teachers College, Columbia University, 1965; Delta paperback, 1966).

Jennings, Frank G. Vacation Reading for the College-Bound. *Family Circle,* July 1965.

Jewett, Arno, Mersand, Joseph, and Gunderson, Doris. Improving English Skills of Culturally Different Youth, OE–30012. United States Office of Education Bulletin 1964, No. 5.

Johnson, Pyke, Jr. Distribution of Paperbound Books. *ALA Bulletin,* June 1963.

Johnson, Pyke, Jr. Mad Tom Books: A Venture in Roadside Selling of Paperbacks. *Publishers' Weekly,* October 5, 1964.

Johnson, Pyke, Jr. Censorship, Critical Thinking and the Paperback. *School Library Journal,* January 15, 1965.

Johnston, Gordon L. Listen to the Mockingbird. *Scholastic Teacher,* January 17, 1964.

Jordon, R. T. Wanted: Paperback Juveniles. *Publishers' Weekly,* November 13, 1961.

Josephs, Lois. Using Paperbacks in Thematic Approaches to Fiction in High School. *Studies in the Mass Media* (NCTE), December 1963.

Kazin, Alfred. How Shall I Read This Book? *The Reporter,* February 1, 1963.

Kebabian, Eleanore. Paperbacks in the [Elementary School] Library. *Scholastic Teacher,* January 17, 1964.

Keeping Pace with the News in Paperbacks: Roundup of Important New Titles. *America,* November 6, 1965.

Kessel, Harlan. Paperbacks Are Books: Book Week News Guest Spot. December 2, 1965, New York *Herald Tribune* Advertising Department.

Klemer, Donald. Salesmanship Seminar for Classroom Libraries. *School Paperback Journal,* November 1964.

Klemer, Donald. Paperbacks . . . for Keeps? *School Paperback Journal,* March 1965.

Klemer, Donald and Sutton, John. Summer Reading Program . . . Some Why's and How's. *School Paperback Journal,* May 1965.

Klingmeyer, F. M. Paperbacks and Hardbacks. *The Clearing House,* March 1960.

Klohn, Louise L. Classroom or School Libraries? *The Clearing House,* February 1959.

Kohler, Wilma B. 100 Outstanding Paperback Books. *The Catholic Educator,* January 1964.

Koneff, Donald. An Experiment in Incentive Learning. *School Paperback Journal,* December 1965.

Kublin, H. Paperbacks on Asia for High School Use. *Social Education,* February 1960.

Kuhn, Eleanor. Paperbacks in the Junior High Library. *Studies in the Mass Media* (NCTE), March 1961.

Kunkle, Hannah J. Junior Book Collectors: A Book Fair with A Twist. *Wilson Library Bulletin,* October 1963.

Kvaraceus, W. Can Reading Affect Delinquency? *ALA Bulletin,* June 1965.

LaBrant, Lou. Lifetime Reading and the Paperback Book. In Butman et al., *Paperbacks in the Schools* (New York: Bantam Books, 1963), pp. 13–22.

Larkin, W. J. Beyond the Text: Paperbacks Vitalize Social Studies, *The Clearing House,* September 1965.

Larrick, Nancy. Letter to Parents. *Scholastic Teacher,* March 4, 1965.

Larrick, Nancy. Summer Reading Programs Pay Big Dividends. *Scholastic Teacher,* March 4, 1965.

Lash, Henry. The Paperback Revolution in the Junior College. *Junior College Journal,* March 1961.

Lash, Henry, and Dellefield, Calvin. Paperbacks and Adult Education. *School Library Journal,* January 15, 1962.

Lash, Henry, and Dellefield, Calvin. Famous People: A Bibliography of Biographies in Paperback Editions (pamphlet). Division of College and Adult Education, Los Angeles, 1965.

Laskey, Harold H. New Paperback Exhibit Program in California Schools. *California School Libraries,* May 1965.

Laskey, Harold H. Paperback Exhibit for Schools. *School Libraries,* January 1964.

Laux, Dean M. Science and Math. *Scholastic Teacher,* December 2, 1964.

Law, R. A. Paperbound Books in English Courses. *Pennsylvania School Journal,* January 1965.

Lee, Elsie J. Serving the Gifted. *School Libraries,* May 1964.

Lee, Norman. Paperback Books for Senior High School English. *Studies in the Mass Media* (NCTE), December 1961.

Leonard, I. A., and Hamill, H. M. Select List of Paperbacks on Latin America. *Hispania,* March 1964.

Light, L. M. Using Paperbacks with Slow Readers. *Chicago Schools Journal,* November 1962.

Litzinger, William D. Paperback Usage in Schools. *The Clearing House,* April 1964.

Lombardo, I. Thematic Approach to Literature Teaching. *Chicago Schools Journal,* October 1962.

Loretan, Joseph O. New Materials for Tomorrow's Education. *Book Production,* November 1964.

Ludington, Jerry. Paperback Bookstores? Here's How! *School Paperback Journal,* October 1964.

McCaffrey, Austin J. What's Ahead in Educational Publishing? *Scholastic Teacher,* November 18, 1965.

McGinniss, Dorothy A. Paperbacks in the School Library. In Butman et al., *Paperbacks in the Schools* (New York: Bantam Books, 1963), pp. 122–130.

McKenzie, L. Religion Syllabus Employing Paperbacks. *Catholic School Journal,* September 1965.

McLaughlin, Frank. Where PBs Replace Textbooks. *Scholastic Teacher,* March 13, 1963.

McLaughlin, Frank. Waiting: The Reluctant Student. *School Paperback Journal,* November 1964.

McLaughlin, Frank. The Old Man and the Sea Comes Home! *School Paperback Journal,* February 1965.

McLaughlin, Frank. Seeing with New Eyes. *School Paperback Journal,* April 1965.

McLaughlin, Frank. Selecting and Defending Controversial Books. *School Paperback Journal*, September 1965.

McLaughlin, Frank. Training To Write through Pictures. *School Paperback Journal*, October 1965.

Madden, Edgar. Popularizing Reading in the Small High School. *English Journal*, January 1963.

Maloney, Henry B. Another Look at Paperbacks. *The Clearing House*, January 1964.

Maloney, Henry B. The Slow Learners Booster Club Needs You. *School Paperback Journal*, November 1965.

Manthorne, Jane. The Supermarket Come-On: A Paperback Experiment with Young Adults. *School Library Journal*, January 15, 1965.

Manual for a Successful Book Fair. *Scholastic Teacher*, February 14, 1964.

Marcus, Fred H. Structure and the Short Story. *Studies in the Mass Media* (NCTE), February 1962.

Martin, Lowell A. Students and the Pratt Library: Challenge and Opportunity (pamphlet). Enoch Pratt Free Library, Baltimore, 1963.

Merrill, J. A. Children's Libraries: Public Library and the School Book Fair. *Wilson Library Bulletin*, June 1965.

Mersand, Joseph. Bibliography; The Use of Paperbacks in the Schools. In Butman et al., *Paperbacks in the Schools* (New York: Bantam Books, 1963), pp. 139–152.

Mersand, Joseph. Reading for Superior Students in a Comprehensive High School. *The Reading Teacher*, May 1963.

Mersand, Joseph. The Aims of English Instruction. *High Points*, January 1965.

Mills, Peter. Shane and Homer Smith: Two Contemporary Legends. *School Paperback Journal*, November 1964.

Modules of Experience for Teaching Science. *West Side News and Morningsider* (Supplement), October 21, 1965.

Moestue, Susan. The Merits of a Paperback Bookshop. *School Paperback Journal*, December 1964.

Montgomery, Iona. Especially for You. *Studies in the Mass Media* (NCTE), March 1961.

Moon, Eric. On the Shelf. *School Library Journal*, January 15, 1964.

Moon, Eric. The View from the Front. *Library Journal*, February 1, 1964.

Moon, Eric. Paperbacks: for Sale? *School Library Journal*, May 15, 1964.

Moscow, David H. Individualizing Classroom Reading. In Butman et al., *Paperbacks in the Schools* (New York: Bantam Books, 1963), pp. 39–49.

Moscow, David H. Paperbacks; A Planned Program for Southfield High School. *Studies in the Mass Media* (NCTE), January 1963.

Moscow, David H. The Paperback Goes to School. *Illinois School Board Journal,* May–June 1963.

Moscow, David H. Individualizing Instruction with Paperbacks. *NEA Journal,* April 1964.

New, George. Paperbounds and Educational Theater. *Paperbound Books in Print,* February 1965.

New Jersey Paperback Study. *Scholastic Teacher,* January 17, 1964.

Newman, R. E. Book Is To Buy: Elementary School Paperback Bookstore. *Saturday Review,* January 16, 1965.

New Professional Books: Issues and Approaches. *Scholastic Teacher,* December 2, 1964.

Newton, David. Teaching Research Techniques with Paperbacks. *School Paperback Journal,* February 1965.

Nissman, Albert. Potpourri on Paperbacks. *Studies in the Mass Media* (NCTE), December 1961.

No, But I Read the Book Twice: Remaining a Book or Putting a Suggestive Cover on Its Dust Jacket. *Christian Century,* January 6, 1965.

Noar, Gertrude. Heroes for Children. *Scholastic Teacher,* October 7, 1964.

Noyes, Judith. Paperbacks for Children Win Sales. *Publishers' Weekly,* July 12, 1965.

Olsen, J. Coming Revolution in Textbooks: Instructional Program Packages. *AV Communication Review,* Fall, 1964.

One-Book Classrooms on Way Out—Carline. *West Side News and Morningsider* (Supplement), October 21, 1965.

O'Neal, Robert. World Literature in High School; Lusty Orphan. *English Journal,* February 1963.

Open Curriculum for High Schools. *West Side News and Morningsider* (Supplement), October 21, 1965.

Paperback Awards in the Schools: A Unique Experiment. *Paperbound Books in Print,* November 1965.

Paperback Books—A Swing around the Country. *School Management,* June 1964.

Paperback Books, Grade School through High School. *Saturday Review,* September 11, 1965.

Paperback Books in Chemistry and Related Sciences. *Journal of Chemical Education,* April 1963, April 1965.

Paperback Books (Teachers College Paperback Conference). *Christian Science Monitor,* October 8, 1965.

Paperback Conference: Success at Columbia. *Scholastic Teacher,* October 28, 1965.

Paperback Cover Designs Are Tasteful and Effective. *Publishers' Weekly,* February 1, 1965.

Paperback Explosion. *Wilson Library Bulletin,* December 1961.

The Paperback Story: Soft-Cover Books Have Begun an Exciting New Chapter. *Barron's,* May 3, 1965.

Paperbacks as Textbooks in Texas: A Tentative No. *Publishers' Weekly,* February 4, 1963.

Paperbacks Boost Chance for Professional Growth. *West Side News and Morningsider* (Supplement), October 21, 1965.

Paperbacks in Libraries; A Symposium. *Wilson Library Bulletin,* May 1963.

Paperbacks in the Bookstore: Report of Discussion at ABA Los Angeles Meeting. *Publishers' Weekly,* October 25, 1965.

Paperbacks in the Home. *West Side News and Morningsider* (Supplement), October 21, 1965.

Paperbacks in the Social Sciences. *Scholastic Teacher,* January 17, 1964.

Paperbacks on Russia Feed Increasing U.S. Appetite. *Michigan Education Journal,* November 1962.

Paperbacks Termed "Proper" in Boston. *Christian Science Monitor,* August 12, 1963.

Paperbacks Widely Used in New Jersey Classrooms: A Report on the New Jersey Study. *American School and University,* October 1965.

Paperbacks Work Magic in Schools, Bogart Says. *West Side News and Morningsider* (Supplement), October 21, 1965.

Pei, Mario. Languages in Paperback: Tool for Education. *Publishers' Weekly,* September 30, 1963; Reply with Rejoinder, G. W. Hubel. *Publishers' Weekly,* October 28, 1963.

Perks, D. M. Paperbacks Preferred. *High Points,* June 1962; November 1962; December 1962; January 1963; February 1963; May 1963; June 1963; November 1963; February 1964; March 1964; May 1964; June 1964; November 1964; April 1965; May 1965; and June 1965.

Pfretzchner, P. A. New Viewpoints and the Paperback. *Social Studies,* April 1960.

Pirolo, Charles A. The $50 Bookshelf. *The Lutheran,* August 26, 1964.

Polos, Nicholas C. Textbooks: What's Wrong with Them? *The Clearing House,* April 1964.

Pony Boom: The Object Is To Pass, Isn't It? *Newsweek,* November 22, 1965.

Public Libraries in Metropolitan Toronto Automate Reordering of Paperbacks. *School Library Journal,* May 15, 1965.

Put Paperbacks to Work for You. *Techniques for Teachers of Adults* (periodical leaflet). National Association of Public School Adult Educators, Washington, D.C.

Rahtz, R. Paperbacks as Textbooks. *Scholastic Teacher,* November 18, 1965.

Rapid Rise of Paperback Textbooks. *Chicago Schools Journal,* January 1962.

Recent Paperback Books for High Schools. *NEA Journal,* September 1965.

Redding, Frank. Revolution in the Textbook Industry (pamphlet).

Dept. of Audio-visual Instruction, National Education Association, Washington, D.C., 1963.

Reed, Cecilia. Ballad of the Reluctant Reader. *School Paperback Journal,* March 1965.

Rehage, K. J. In Paper Covers. *Elementary School Journal,* November 1961.

Reilly, Frank. A Paperback Book Club. *School Management,* August 1962.

Revolution in Paperbacks Nowhere Near Classroom, Abraham Lass Charges. *West Side News and Morningsider* (Supplement), October 21, 1965.

Riccio, Richard. Those Who Won't Will! *School Paperback Journal,* November 1965.

Rice, Frank A. Language Books in Paperbacks. *The Linguistic Reporter* (Newsletter of the Center for Applied Linguistics, Modern Language Association), October 1963.

Richards, Vincent. The Cheap Paperback Is No Country Cousin. In de Grazia and Sohn (Eds.), *Revolution in Teaching: New Theory, Technology, and Curricula* (New York: Bantam Books, 1964), pp. 145–151.

Richards, Vincent. Paperbacks in Canada. *School Paperback Journal,* May 1965.

Richards, William. A Pocketful of Classics. *Scholastic Teacher,* December 2, 1964.

Richardson, Jean. Paperbacks for Educators. *Scholastic Teacher,* October 28, 1965.

Rioux, J. W. Nine Tested Reasons for Using Paperback Books. *The Nation's Schools,* November 1962.

Roberts, Richard E. From Hard Cover to Soft. *Studies in the Mass Media* (NCTE), March 1961.

Robertson, Nan. Paperback Books Gain Stature with Increased Use in Schools. *New York Times,* October 5, 1961.

Rogers, Marjorie L. The Use of Paperbacks by a School System. *Ohio Library Association Bulletin,* April 1963.

The Role of Paperback Books in Education Examined in Depth (Report on the Teachers College Conference). *Publishers' Weekly,* November 1, 1965.

The Role of the Paperback in Science Teaching (Report on the Teachers College Conference). *Publishers' Weekly,* November 15, 1965.

Ross, Frank E. For the Disadvantaged Student—A Program that Swings. *English Journal,* April 1965.

Ross, Frank E. Teaching the 3 R's. *School Paperback Journal,* November 1965.

Rossoff, Martin. *The Library in High School Teaching* (New York: H. W. Wilson, 1961).

Rossoff, Martin. How School Library Paperbacks Meet Reading and Research Needs. *Scholastic Teacher,* March 13, 1963.

Rossoff, Martin. Using Your High School Library, 2nd ed. (New York: H. W. Wilson, 1964).

Rothman, I. N. Paperback in the Classroom. *Educational Forum,* January 1965.

Rouse, John J. Paperbacks and English Programs in High School. *Studies in the Mass Media* (NCTE), January 1963.

Rouse, John J. Team Teaching and the English Program. *School Paperback Journal,* April 1965.

Rouse, John J. As a Matter of Fact! *School Paperback Journal,* October 1965.

Ruhnke, E. Supplementary Reading. *School Management,* August 1962.

Russ, L. Juvenile Paperbacks or the Curious Case of Curious George. *Publishers' Weekly,* March 15, 1964.

Sanders, James L. Professional Education Library in Paperbacks. *Arizona Teacher,* May 1965; *Phi Delta Kappan,* October 1965; and *Paperbound Books in Print,* October 1965.

Sanders, Father James W., S.J. Soft Covered Culture: The Paperback in High School. *The Catholic Educator,* November 1959.

Schick, Frank L. *The Paperbound Book in America* (New York: R. R. Bowker, 1959).

Schick, Frank L. New Dimensions in Paperbacks. *Paperbound Books in Print,* Summer, 1963.

Schiller, Hillel. Panel Urges Schools To Incorporate Paperbacks; Striking Cases Cited. *School Library Journal,* February 15, 1963.

Schoenbaum, S. Elizabethan and Jacobean Plays: The New Paperbacks. *College English,* October 1964.

School and Bookstore: An Experiment with Surprises. *Publishers' Weekly,* July 13, 1964.

The School Bookstore, Book Fair, and the Local Paperback Distributor. In Butman et al., *Paperbacks in the Schools* (New York: Bantam Books, 1963), pp. 131–138.

A Schoolman's Guide to Paperback Bookstores. *School Management,* August 1962.

Schools Are Taking a Second Look at the Pupil and the Paperback: A Report on the New Jersey Study. *Book Production Industry,* September 1965.

Scoggin, Margaret C. First Catch Your Hare. *ALA Bulletin,* January 1959.

Searles, John R. More Sources of Free and Inexpensive Material. *English Journal,* September 1965 and previous years.

Selected Lists of Paperbacks on Shakespeare. *Christian Century,* April 15, 1964.

Selectivity vs Censorship. *West Side News and Morningsider* (Supplement), October 21, 1965.

Shakespeare or Salinger? *West Side News and Morningsider* (Supplement), October 21, 1965.

Shakin, Grace M. Six Books for Two Bucks: Paperbacks in the Elementary School Library. *School Library Journal* (Children's Section), January 15, 1963.

Shatzkin, Leonard. The Book in Search of a Reader. *Daedalus,* Winter, 1963.

Shefter, Harry. Free Paperbacks Can Help Stem Cost of Education. *West Side News and Morningsider* (Supplement), October 21, 1965.

Shute, D. C. The Case of the Paperback Texts. *Illinois Education,* December 1959.

Sieben, J. Kenneth. Terminal Student . . . Emerging Citizen. *School Paperback Journal,* November 1965.

Sister Avila. Pioneering in Paperbacks. *Scholastic Teacher,* March 13, 1963.

Sister Catherine Virginia. Using Paperbacks with Science Classes. *Catholic School Journal,* February 1964.

Sister Joseph Kevin. Paperbacks in a Book Fair on Wheels. *Catholic School Journal,* October 1964.

Sister M. Clarencia. I Sing of the Paperback. *The Catholic Educator,* September 1962.

Sister M. Clarencia. 150 Outstanding Paperbacks. *The Catholic Educator,* January 1965.

Sister Marie Cecile. Library's Role in the Educative Process. *The Catholic Educator,* April 1963.

Sister Mary Alician. Paperbacks; Mirror for Adolescents. *The Clearing House,* March 1962.

Sister Mary Alician. Mining the Paperback. *The Catholic Educator,* April 1963.

Sister Mary Francis Romana. We Had a Paperback Book Fair. *The Catholic Educator,* September 1962.

Sister Mary Paul. Paperbacks Promote Use of the Library. *Catholic School Journal,* February 1963.

Sister Mary Sylvia. Cyrano—The Knight of the White Plume. *School Paperback Journal,* April 1965.

Sister St. Agnes. Developing the Critical-Minded Catholic Student: The Current Trend in Paperback Books. *National Catholic Educational Association Bulletin,* August 1961.

Six Easy Lessons. *Scholastic Teacher,* May 15, 1964.

Smallenburg, C. and H. Should We Censor What Adolescents Read? (with Study Discussion Program). *PTA Magazine,* March 1965.

Smith, Cordelia. I Want It To Come Home To. *Top of the News* (ALA), May 1964.

Smith, G. R. Summer Reading Lists for Secondary Schools: with Yale Co-op's List of Paperbacks. *Publishers' Weekly,* September 27, 1965.

Smith, Roger H. (Ed.) *The American Reading Public: A Symposium* (New York: R. R. Bowker, 1964).

Smith, Roger H. Paperback Distribution: Booksellers and Wholesalers. *Publishers' Weekly,* November 9, 1964.

Sohn, David A. The Stimulation of Reading through Paperback Books; The Classroom Library. In Butman et al., *Paperbacks in the Schools* (New York: Bantam Books, 1963), pp. 23–38.

Sohn, David A. Paperbacks in Classroom. *Scholastic Teacher,* January 17, 1964.

Sohn, David A. New York City Schools Welcome Paperbacks. *School Paperback Journal,* October 1964.

Sohn, David A. The Classroom Library Sparks a Chain Reaction. *School Paperback Journal,* December 1964.

Sohn, David A. Paperbacks in the Language Arts. *School Paperback Journal,* April 1965.

Solak, Marilyn. Shall We Read This Summer? *School Paperback Journal,* May 1965.

Solomon, Stanley. Paperback Bonanza. *Scholastic Teacher,* March 15, 1961.

Soule, Gardner. Book Censors: What To Do about Them. *Scholastic Teacher,* October 7, 1964.

Spiegler, Charles G. If Only Dickens Had Written about Hot Rods. *English Journal,* April 1965.

Sprague, Jane. Paper-Bound Books Fine Class Aid. *New York World–Telegram and Sun,* October 26, 1965.

Statistics on Paperback Books. *Education U.S.A.,* October 14, 1965.

Steinhauber, Harry. Foreign Language Paperbacks. In Butman et al., *Paperbacks in the Schools* (New York: Bantam Books, 1963), pp. 112–121.

Stocker, Hilda L. Paperbacks in the Classroom. *School Library Journal* (Children's Section), January 15, 1964.

The Story of the New American Library of World Literature, Inc. *Book Production Magazine,* June 1964.

The Students' Right To Read (pamphlet). National Council of Teachers of English, Champaign, Ill., 1962.

Survey Finds Wide Use of Paperbacks. *American School and University,* October 1965.

Takagi, K. K. Books at the Crossroads. *International Journal of Religious Education,* October 1964.

Talbot, Ross B. Paperbacks and Politics. *The Educational Paperback Researcher,* Volume 3, Jacksonville, Ill.

Taylor: Beyond the Cultural Cage. *West Side News and Morningsider* (Supplement), October 21, 1965.

Teachers Lead Revolt on Textbook Tyranny. *West Side News and Morningsider* (Supplement), October 21, 1965.

Tebbel, John. Paperback Textbook Revolution. *Saturday Review,* March 11, 1961.

Tebbel, John. Paperbacks: Revolution or Evolution? *Saturday Review,* June 13, 1964.

Teen-Agers Can Be Readers: An NLW Conference on Teen-Age Reading. *Publishers' Weekly,* November 30, 1959.

Terminal Students, Anyone? *School Paperback Journal,* November 1965.

Tesovnik, Mary. Paperbacks. *Milwaukee Reader,* March 30, 1964.

Textbook Selection: Whose Job? *School Management,* April 1964.

Thomson, J. Children's Paperbacks. *School Library Journal,* May 15, 1965.

Tower, Jay. Libraries, Students, Paperbacks. *School Library Journal* (Children's Section), January 15, 1963.

A Treasury of Important, Recent Paperbacks for High Schools. *NEA Journal,* September 1965.

Tresize, Joan Lenon. Plan for Critical Reading. *School Libraries,* May 1965.

Two Faces of the Chicago Tribune: Controversy over James Baldwin's "Another Country" as College Required Reading. *Christian Century,* February 3, 1965.

Tyre, Richard. The Private School: Paradise for the Paperback. *School Paperback Journal,* December 1964.

Van Buren, A. Survival. *School Management,* August 1962.

Vedro, Alfred. Shades of Jules Verne and H. G. Wells. *School Paperback Journal,* February 1965.

Virtue of Paperbacks in Curriculum Is Cited. *West Side News and Morningsider* (Supplement), October 21, 1965.

Walker, G. L. Bring on the Paperbacks. *Catholic School Journal,* May 1963.

Walker, Jerry L. New Literature for Adolescents. *Scholastic Teacher,* January 17, 1964.

Warner, J. F. Anthologies in the High School Classroom? *English Journal,* October 1959.

Warner, J. F. To the Gallows with You, Miss Zilch. *English Journal,* December 1960.

Watts, Doris R. Not Whether, But How . . . . *Scholastic Teacher,* March 13, 1963.

Watts, Doris R. The Public Library and the Teen-Age. *Wilson Library Bulletin,* November 1963.

Watts, Doris R. Library and the Teen Age: Concerning College Preparatory Reading List by Nioga Library System. *Wilson Library Bulletin,* May 1964.

Weiss, M. Jerry. *Reading in the Secondary Schools* (New York: Odyssey Press, 1961).

Weiss, M. Jerry. Paperbacks in Elementary Schools. *The Instructor*, March 1962.

Weiss, M. Jerry. 1962 Potpourri on Paperbacks. *Studies in the Mass Media* (NCTE), January 1963.

Weiss, M. Jerry. Paperback Projects in the News. *Studies in the Mass Media* (NCTE), December 1963.

West, Marcia. Communication in Science Teaching. *School Paperback Journal*, February 1965.

What Books for the Young Adult? Publisher Asks, Librarian Answers. *School Library Journal*, October 15, 1964.

What Role for Paperbacks in Schools. *Book Production*, December 1964.

What School Officials Say about Paperback Stores. *School Management* magazine's *Research Report*, April 2, 1962.

What Your District Can Do about School Libraries. *School Management*, April 1964.

Where the Money Lies. *Time*, March 12, 1965.

Whitmer, Dana P. When Someone Complains. *Scholastic Teacher*, January 17, 1964.

Wilson, Pauline. Hot Potato Produces Cool Discussion. *Top of the News* (ALA), May 1964.

Wolfe, I. How Children Build Personal Libraries in Tenafly. *Scholastic Teacher*, January 17, 1964.

Wofford, Azile. *Book Selection for School Libraries* (New York: H. W. Wilson, 1962).

Wonnberger, Carl. Shakespeare in Paperback. *Scholastic Teacher* (Special Shakespeare Issue), February 21, 1964.

Woods, George A. Paperbacks Go to School. *New York Times Book Review* (Paperback Book Section), January 5, 1964.

Wysocki, Mary. Paperbacks in Elementary Schools. *Studies in the Mass Media* (NCTE), December 1961.

You Can't Judge a Textbook. *The Insider's Newsletter for Women* (Cowles Magazines), January 1, 1962.

Yungmeyer, Elinor. Cooperation in Action. *ALA Bulletin*, September 1965.

Zamchick, David. The Arts and Humanities. *Scholastic Teacher*, January 17, 1964 and December 2, 1964.

Zamchick, David. Paperback Buying Patterns. *English Journal*, May 1960.